Making It

ALSO BY LOUIS UCHITELLE

The Disposable American: Layoffs and Their Consequences

Making It

WHY MANUFACTURING
STILL MATTERS

Louis Uchitelle

THE NEW PRESS

25 YEARS

NEW YORK
LONDON

Requests for permission to reproduce selections from this book should be mailed to:
Permissions Department, The New Press, 120 Wall Street, 31st floor,
New York, NY 10005.

Published in the United States by The New Press, New York, 2017
Distributed by Perseus Distribution

ISBN 978-1-59558-897-5 (hc)
ISBN 978-1-62097-101-7 (e-book)

CIP data is available

The New Press publishes books that promote and enrich public discussion and
understanding of the issues vital to our democracy and to a more equitable
world. These books are made possible by the enthusiasm of our readers; the support
of a committed group of donors, large and small; the collaboration of our many
partners in the independent media and the not-for-profit sector; booksellers, who
often hand-sell New Press books; librarians; and above all by our authors.

www.thenewpress.com

Composition by Westchester Publishing Services
This book was set in Fairfield

Printed in the United States of America

2   4   6   8   10   9   7   5   3   1

For my wife, Joan Uchitelle, who
anchors our lives in wonderful ways
and
My brother Ben, whose steady
encouragement made this book possible

Contents

Preface

Twenty years ago, in 1987, two academic economists—Stephen S. Cohen and John Zysman, colleagues at the University of California, Berkeley—called attention to the importance of manufacturing for the national well-being. Their book, *Manufacturing Matters: The Myth of the Post-industrial Economy*, warned against overreliance on the service sector, no matter how sophisticated and robust that sector was and is. Their warning went unheeded. Manufacturing plays even less of a role in the American economy, and in our lives, than it did in 1987, but it still matters, very much. I decided to make that point in the title of this book. There is no getting off the hook. Any doubts about that have been largely swept aside by the election of Donald J. Trump, who came to office with the pivotal support of people damaged by manufacturing's shrunken presence in the United States.

Louis Uchitelle
February 2017

Acknowledgments

This book comes out of years of reporting for the *New York Times*, and then more reporting to tell the story, with as many specifics as possible, of manufacturing's shrunken role in the American economy. This is not a "gotcha" tale. Many of the insights came from top executives of the multinational corporations that dominate manufacturing in the United States, and put factories abroad rather than rely mainly on exports to serve foreign markets. Jeffrey Immelt, chairman and chief executive of General Electric, was particularly informative. He sat for several interviews and made others in his organization available to me, among them Richard Kennedy, a public relations officer in GE's Cincinnati office, who arranged key interviews and visits.

Over the course of reporting and writing this book, I spoke frequently with Tom Geoghegan, a labor lawyer in Chicago and a prolific author. His suggestions and criticisms improved the manuscript, and his enthusiasm helped to keep me going. My brother Ben Uchitelle was similarly supportive. After law school, he settled in St. Louis, and during the course of his career he served three terms as mayor of Clayton, a near-in suburb. His good reputation opened numerous doors for me in the reporting for chapter 3, which focuses on urban manufacturing. So did that of his wife, Susan Uchitelle, an activist and educator. I stayed with them on my reporting trips to St. Louis, and Ben and I grew close again as brothers, as we had been as boys. My sister, Elizabeth Zinner, also provided considerable encouragement.

I am particularly indebted to my editors at the New Press—Marc Favreau above all, as well as Emily Albarillo and Sarah Fan. This book would not have made it to publication without Marc's excellent editing and quiet, steady encouragement. That is also true of Glenn Kramon, business editor at the *New York Times* during my early years there as an economics reporter, and Steve Prokesch, enterprise editor in the department during those same years. Their enthusiasm for my work encouraged me to include manufacturing as a major theme for an economics writer, taking the beat beyond its usual focus on Federal Reserve policy, economic growth rates, inflation, and the like.

My daughters, Isabel Finegold and Jennifer Weinberg, who live nearby, were always supportive, as were their husbands, and their four children. The latter, particularly the younger ones, would come into my study on their frequent visits, ask me what chapter I was writing, and cheer when I told them I had moved on from the chapter I had been writing on their last visit. Or moan in mock disappointment when I hadn't moved on. Their good-natured prodding helped to keep me moving forward. I wanted to report progress to them.

Many others helped in the birth of this book. They included numerous men and women—particularly factory workers—whose jobs had disappeared and whose hourly pay had shrunk, if they could get new work at all. It was from them that I first heard the view that their children might not do as well as they had. Such pessimism was startling to my ears, as I had grown up during and just after World War II, when most Americans, including factory workers— especially factory workers—assumed that their children would reach a higher rung in life. Upward mobility was a given.

This book is embedded in data, most of it compiled by government agencies. Early in my years as an economics writer for the *New York Times*, I discovered how readily available this data was and how forthcoming government employees were in sharing it with journalists and, through them, the public. Such openness was particularly true of the Bureau of Labor Statistics, the Bureau of Economic Analysis, and the Census Bureau. While I gathered some of the data myself from these agencies and from others, I turned repeatedly to people more adept than I at locating and tapping databases. In this regard, I am particularly grateful to Seth Feaster, Aaron Freedman, and Jessica Huseman for their crucial research assistance.

Numerous others provided information and insights, among them Manuel Weinberg, the father-in-law of one of my daughters, who owned a small manufacturing business in Connecticut; Ruth Keenoy, a historical preservation specialist in St. Louis whose generous assistance and knowledge contributed immeasurably to the chapter on urban manufacturing; and Jeff Madrick, a colleague and friend whose sensible advice over many years, and whose own writing, helped to shape this book. I also learned over the years from Dean Baker, Ronald Blackwell, Steven Capozzola, Eileen Appelbaum, Kim Didier, Robert Baugh, Jared Bernstein, Josh Bivens, Robert Combs, Kenneth N. Davis Jr., the late Fred S. Epstein, Jerry Jasinowski, Sean P. McAlinden, Jason L. Furman, Susan N. Helper, Susan

Houseman, Madeline Janis, William C. Lane, Ronald Lazar, Brian Lombardozzi, David Leonhardt, Daniel Luria, Richard A. McCormack, Sean P. McAlinden, Paul Nettler, Gordon Pavy, Tom Redburn, and Dana Spitzer.

Finally, I am indebted to my wife, Joan Uchitelle, a constant source of support and encouragement. We are companions in a long and satisfying life together.

Making It

1

The Long Unwinding

Most Americans no longer pay much attention to factories. They assume there aren't that many still in operation in the United States—not in a country where people are more likely to see empty, boarded-up buildings that once were engines of manufacturing. Nor is there much awareness of the ingenious ways in which factories function.[1] True, we lament outsourcing and are uneasy about the country's huge trade deficit. We are troubled that so much of what we purchase, and need, is made overseas. But we are less and less troubled as the years pass. We even import, without acknowledging the irony, most of the machines that are installed in the factories we have—machines that stamp a sheet of steel into an auto fender, for example, or bore cylinder holes into iron or aluminum-alloy engine blocks. Take away the imported machinery, and most of our factories would resemble nearly empty, cavernous warehouses. Or leave the imported machinery in place, but take away the imported parts that go into so many products made in our factories, and those products would become unusable. Auto dashboards, for example, might still be labeled Made in America, but absent imported components, many would come off assembly lines grossly disfigured, with round, empty holes into which foreign-made gauges were previously implanted.

In terms of factory output, no nation in the world other than China produces more than the United States. Standard government statistics are clear on this point, although they are also misleading.[2] Within manufacturing, a relatively small sector—the production of computers, electronics, and related products—accounts for most of the output growth. In addition, the manufacturing base in the United States (that is, the number of companies operating factories in the country) is narrow. If the U.S.-based multinationals— the GEs, the GMs, the IBMs, the Dow Chemicals—were to shut their American plants and transfer production to their numerous factories overseas, exporting back to the United States what they now make here, we would cease to be a manufacturing nation of consequence:[3] fully two-thirds of what is manufactured in the United States is produced by the U.S.-based factories of American-owned multinationals.[4] Of course, in this fantasy scenario, thousands of small manufacturers would continue to operate in this country, but many of them make the parts that go into what the multinationals produce in their U.S. factories. Without the latter, the ranks of the smaller fry would be diminished.

If we look back to the 1950s and 1960s, we see an era in which U.S. domestic manufacturers large and small made nearly *all* of the finished products that Americans purchased, as well as the component parts and materials used to make those products, and most of the machinery used to fashion the parts and materials into those finished products. Yet even this golden age undercounted manufacturing's vast presence in the U.S. economy. Undetected by the federal government's statistical radar, legions of brokers and dealers moved the manufacturing process along, arranging to get raw materials to factories, semi-finished products to the next stage of production, and finished products to warehouses, showrooms, and stores.

Those middlemen included people like my father, who in the early and mid-twentieth century acted as brokers or sales agents for the numerous textile manufacturers in the United States, finding buyers for the millions of yards of newly woven cloth then flowing from their factories. The buyers were other manufacturers, also still located in the United States, who dyed the cloth, or cut and sewed it, once it was dyed, into sheets or aprons or dish towels or tablecloths or shirts or socks or summer-weight pants or curtains or the numerous other products that were made from cotton in the years before rayon, nylon, and other synthetics were widely adopted. For all the flow from one factory to the next, however, the factory owners rarely orchestrated this process themselves. They outsourced that function to brokers such as my father, who collected commissions on each inter-factory transaction. Yet the brokers' often middle-class incomes for performing this essential function were not usually counted in government data as manufacturing income. If that had been the case, then manufacturing's statistical share of the gross domestic product (GDP) would have been noticeably higher than the official post–World War II peak of 28.9 percent in 1953. (Instead, the brokers' and dealers' earnings were counted as wholesale income.) And the fall from that peak, to 12 percent in 2014, might have drawn more attention to the thwarted lives of thousands of college-educated young people who followed their fathers into family businesses as brokers and dealers and, ten or fifteen years later, found themselves out of work.

My father, not suspecting what lay ahead, offered the manufacturing path to his three sons, who graduated from college in the 1950s. As a self-employed cotton "gray goods" broker, he facilitated the movement of newly woven cloth (grayish or off-white in color) to the next manufacturer in the process. If we joined him, he said, he would do more than just facilitate the launch of our careers: he would step into the production chain himself, leasing or purchasing a textile mill. Meanwhile, he competed with other brokers to find buyers for cloth as it rolled out of the country's mills. While the buyers he served were mainly dyers, he also brokered the sale of dyed cloth, although not as often. Gray goods were his specialty. His standard commission was 0.5 percent of the transaction price, a small cut indeed, but one that swelled into an upper middle-class income over the course of many, many brokered transactions.

Occasionally my father took a risk. Instead of acting as a broker, he would buy gray goods himself—thousands of yards of cloth, using a line of credit—and quickly resell it to a manufacturer who dyed or printed a pattern on the cloth. That way he collected the markup rather than the smaller commission. "Taking a position," he called this maneuver, and risking a loss. I suppose he must have taken some losses, although he rarely admitted to one, at least not to his sons.

For us, he would acquire a factory so we could earn a profit from actually making cloth, not just brokering the manufacturing process. He imagined that the factory he purchased or leased would weave thread into gray goods, that being the stage of production that interested him most. He assured us, his sons, that we would not have to move to the town where this factory was located. We could operate instead from lower Manhattan, where brokers such as my father and a number of manufacturers had offices, and periodically visit our factory, which would be run day-to-day by foremen and managers. In the end, we turned him down, mainly because owning or even leasing a factory was his vision, not ours. Moreover, he was not an easy man to work with, at least not for his sons. We moved on, my older brother and I into journalism and our younger brother into law, not realizing until twenty years later that if we had followed our father into an expanded family textile business, we would have found ourselves scrambling, in our early forties, for other ways to make a living as the industry that he wanted to bequeath to us moved overseas.

The textile factories that had flourished in America—those that spun raw cotton into thread, those that wove the thread into cloth on giant, noisy looms, and those that dyed or printed fabric—had been located mostly in New England's cities and large towns before World War II and mostly in the less-expensive South afterward, in the period when my father was hoping to draw his sons into the business. Garment manufacturers too migrated southward in a similar pattern after the war, but more than a few lingered in northern cities, two reasons being the skilled workers that urban areas offered and the proximity to department stores and other big retailers, when shopping for clothes and linens was still done mainly in midtown emporiums.

New York City in my father's era had many garment factories, some of them within walking distance of his office at 40 Worth Street, in lower Manhattan. A few were clients and, when I came to his office as a teenager, he would occasionally take me with him on a factory visit. While he schmoozed with owners and salesmen in the front offices, a secretary or clerk, as a courtesy, walked me back into the huge, loft-like factory spaces behind the offices, where I watched cutters and sewers at work making pants, jackets, shirts, and other pieces of clothing. Their skill and dexterity fascinated me and, playing on my awe, they would offer to let me cut three or four layers of fabric, admonishing me to follow the contours of a pattern for a pants leg or a jacket sleeve. I tried, but in wielding the industrial scissors I lacked the skill for a rapid and accurate cut. That came only with experience, and New York enjoyed a large population of experienced garment workers.

There was work for them, at reasonable pay, until the industry shifted out of New York.[5] Some moved with the factories to New England and the South, only to find themselves stranded again, as the migration continued, to Mexico and Asia. Others retrained for entirely different work in other fields outside manufacturing, but most didn't manage to make the transition. The work in other fields went instead to younger people already skilled in these different occupations or more adept at learning them. What happened to factory workers in New York wasn't unique, of course. The same experience played out in the 1980s and 1990s wherever urban manufacturing had once flourished, in many cities and towns east of the Mississippi River.

In that heyday no one talked of skills shortages in manufacturing, not as long as the demand for factory-made merchandise exceeded the supply. Somehow enough skilled workers were found to fill the jobs, or factories hired unskilled men and women and trained them. The issue arose as factories closed in the 1980s and thousands of people who wanted decent-paying factory jobs could no longer find them. The jobs ceased to exist while the workers who wanted them remained, and we were reluctant to acknowledge the shortfall. Instead we put the blame on the unemployed workers themselves, arguing in an epidemic of magical thinking that sophisticated, cutting-edge factories would emerge to replace offshored industries, but only if the unemployed acquired the skills to staff them.[6] New factories did materialize, but not often enough in the United States. The skills needed to staff them, it turned out, existed (or could be acquired easily enough) in Asia and Latin America as well. American manufacturers, as a result, put more and more factories in those parts of the world and equipped them with sophisticated technologies. They did so not only to take advantage of labor pools with appropriate skills but because the demand for manufactured goods rose faster abroad—especially in Asia—than in the United States. In addition, governments on those continents offered subsidies—often generous ones. They recognized something that should have been axiomatic in every country, including the United States: manufacturing is not exclusively a market-dependent activity, and it rarely has been. The process of making physical products is too complicated, too capital intensive, and too dependent on costly and continuous innovation to pay for itself simply from a manufacturer's own, sometimes uncertain, revenues. Governments must supply subsidies in one form or another to sustain this vital activity, and they do so.

We hesitate to call them subsidies, and that reluctance has worked against manufacturing in the United States. While most other industrial nations acknowledge their essential role, we hold back and in doing so allow what are in effect subsidies to be disbursed in haphazard ways. Rather than channel them to manufacturers who export their products, for example, or who bring production home from abroad—adding to the nation's total factory output—we stand by as our cities and towns auction themselves off to manufacturers searching for factory sites, even if a new site is only a few cities away from the old factory and simply replaces production in the old plant rather than increasing it by much. That process spreads more than $80 billion a year across numerous manufacturers.[7] Add to that the nearly $300 billion in annual Defense Department spending, which is really a subsidy dedicated to the manufacture of weapons and other war materiel, and the total is one-sixth of the value of what all of the nation's factories produce each year. Yet public funding of manufacturing does not stop there. We must include the numerous ad hoc subsidies that big manufacturers manage to obtain from all levels of government, offering the often legitimate argument that without such funds, they could not make enough profit to justify staying in business or operating a factory in a particular locale. In total, the flow of public money approaches 20 percent of the value generated in the manufacturing process.

The Revere Copper Company in Rome, New York, for example, has purchased from the New York State government, at cost, the huge quantity of electricity it needs to manufacture copper. This discount from the state power authority's standard price has contributed significantly to Revere's profitability. Similarly, in Louisville, Kentucky, the more than seven hundred employees at General Electric's factory complex there paid a 2-percent wage tax imposed by the city government, which then rebated the money to GE. That's a subsidy funded by GE's own workers! And in Midland, Michigan, the Dow Chemical Company in 2013 opened a battery factory that cost $300 million to construct and equip. Because the batteries were designed to power electric car engines, the federal government paid much of the factory's construction costs, with the justification that battery-powered vehicles were more likely to result in a greener environment than gasoline-powered ones.[8]

Manufacturing in the United States, in sum, is a publicly subsidized market activity. It thrives when the subsidies are generous and well targeted and when the citizenry understands their importance. That is the case in Germany, where manufacturing output has generated a steady 22 percent of the national income year after year for at least seventeen years, and the government is quite open about its participation. In the United States, by contrast, manufacturing's share of GDP in that same period declined from 17 percent in 1998 to 12.1 percent in 2015, in part because our prevailing economic ideology blinds us to the way manufacturing really works in a modern economy, and we hold back on the public support that it requires.[9] In no other industrial nation except Britain and Canada is so little of the economy devoted to manufacturing. The typical range of the sector's share of GDP is between 15 percent (Russia) and 19 percent (Japan), with China and South Korea far above, at 32 percent and 31 percent, respectively.[10] If manufacturing is the defining characteristic of an industrial nation, then the United States is gradually, imperceptibly retreating from that status for lack of a targeted, coordinated subsidy program.

We lament the lure of lower-wage labor overseas, but in fact the lure of subsidies offered by foreign governments frequently plays a more important role in a corporation's decision to put a factory abroad rather than to expand production in the United States and export from home. The Vermeer Corporation of Pella, Iowa, for example, produces horizontal drilling equipment at its factories in Pella for the U.S. market and for export to countries everywhere in the world except China. Among other uses, the company's unique drills offer an efficient way to hollow out horizontal tunnels a few feet below ground level to house power lines running through pipes inserted in the tunnels. The Chinese government, trying to develop a similar machine, insisted that Vermeer put a factory in China rather than export the drills from Iowa, and Vermeer complied in 2008, not wanting to give up the huge market there.

Vermeer in the early years of the twenty-first century earned nearly one-third of its more than $500 million in annual revenue from exports, counting on the U.S. government for trade agreements, favorable currency arrangements, and even white-knuckle diplomacy so that exports would flow smoothly. In China, none of these tactics was sufficient. For several years, Vermeer had been running into competition from a Chinese manufacturer of horizontal drills, who had Chinese government support in the form of free land, tax breaks, and cheap credit, among other subsidies. With its share of this important market falling precipitously, Vermeer opened a factory in Beijing, taking a Chinese partner and soon attracting subsidies for the venture from the Chinese government. Still, the decision to manufacture in China rather than export from the United States was an about-face for Mary Vermeer Andringa, chairwoman of the company her father had founded. "I am a very big proponent of making the United States a great place from which to export," she told me when I interviewed her in 2011 in Pella, where Vermeer has its headquarters and most of its domestic factories. At the time she was also chairwoman of the National Association of Manufacturers (NAM), which should push the eleven thousand companies that are its members to keep their factories in the United States, but doesn't. Over the last thirty years, too many NAM members have located factories abroad. The NAM, as a result, officially favors free trade, which means no subsidies or tariffs that give one nation an advantage over another or hinder a multinational from selling in the United States what it makes in Asia.

Still, as Andringa discovered, free trade is in practice often neutered (see chapter 4). President Barack Obama and his counterparts abroad would have been better off during his eight years in office negotiating trade agreements that acknowledged the essential role played by subsidies in the manufacturing of just about everything that is or could be traded. They would have done well moreover to set official targets for the percentage of GDP from manufacturing that each nation seeks to achieve. In the United States, that would mean a return to a level of 17 percent or even higher, if we as voters bang our fists and insist.

That seems unlikely, given the year-after-year decline in the number of American factory workers, diluting their clout. Automation has shrunk the workforce needed to operate a modern factory, and while output keeps rising, it doesn't rise rapidly enough to result in the rehiring of idled workers, much less recruiting new ones. Recessions and offshoring have also suppressed hiring, reinforcing the employment decline. As a result, jobs in manufacturing reached a historical peak of 19.5 million in June 1979 and have been disappearing ever since, despite occasional upward bumps.[11] The severe recession of the early 1980s accelerated the decline. More jobs disappeared as the nation's factory owners increased their practice of locating factories overseas, lured by subsidies, of course, but also by the growing overseas demand for their products, especially in Asia.

Manufacturing employment in the United States, as a result, had trended downward to 17.3 million jobs by the late 1990s. And then, in the opening years of the twenty-first century, the number, plotted as a line on a chart, plummeted almost as steeply as a waterfall before leveling out in the current decade at around 12 million.[12] The low point—11.5 million men and women—came in 2010, during President Obama's first term, after which an improving, post-recession economy slowly reversed the decline. By midway through Obama's second term, 700,000 jobs had been restored, a gain the president focused on in his public speeches, never mentioning that the improvement was barely noticeable when plotted on a graph stretching back thirty-seven years.[13] In a little more than a single generation, the graph showed, 7 million manufacturing jobs had ceased to exist. The idled workers often found themselves blamed for their plight, for their reputed lack of up-to-date skills. No wonder then that so many people, particularly in the blue-collar workforce, got discouraged and withdrew from the job market. That withdrawal was reflected in the percentage of the adult population actually holding jobs or "actively" seeking employment, a statistic the Department of Labor's Bureau of Labor Statistics has tracked since 1948. After rising for decades, as more and more women and African Americans found jobs, the aptly dubbed "labor force participation rate" finally leveled off in the late 1980s at a strong 66 to 67 percent, and stayed there for nearly twenty years, until 1998, when a new decline began and soon accelerated, plunging the participation rate to not quite 63 percent in 2015.[14]

That is an astonishing drop—indeed, the most prolonged since World War II—and most of it has taken place in manufacturing, where employment fell to 12.3 million in 2016 from 18 million in 1989. As factories have closed, or stayed open but with fewer workers, millions of laid-off workers have dropped out of the U.S. workforce, neither holding nor seeking jobs. They survived on severance payments, reduced pensions, a spouse's salary, and help from their children, many of whom are employed in jobs outside manufacturing that have never paid as well as factory work often does. When I first started visiting factories in the 1980s as an economics writer for the *New York Times*, the line workers often told me that their children would "do better" than they had, by which they meant would earn more. That did not often happen, and gradually the expression—and the expectation—have both disappeared.

The last two decades of the twentieth century were still salad days for factory employment. By 2015, however, nearly one-third of the jobs in manufacturing had disappeared and, as a result, the labor force participation rate for the nation as a whole had fallen back to its 1978 level. Why "participate" when so many well-paying factory jobs—nearly 5 million in 16 years—had vanished, shrinking an entryway to well-paid employment not only on assembly lines but in front offices as well?

The victims in the front offices included several of my boyhood friends whose fathers had owned factories in New York City. After graduating from college, the sons had joined the family business. They did well for a while, but by the early 1970s lower-priced merchandise imported from Asia and Latin America had squeezed them out. One or two succeeded in other lines of work, particularly in real estate, but others struggled to stay employed and never earned as much as their fathers had—a cruel irony, given that the sons had college degrees and many of the fathers did not. Those degrees should have equipped them to understand why they had lost the family business. Instead, like so many others, college educated or not, they blamed lower labor costs overseas, excessive regulation, product piracy, and so on—in their anger skipping over the role that government might have played in facilitating U.S. domestic production, including theirs, instead of letting so much of it slip abroad or simply disappear.

Government had facilitated U.S. manufacturing going back two centuries to the construction of the Erie Canal in the early 1800s. Bonds sponsored by New York State paid for most of the canal's construction and, after its completion, factories sprang up along its route.[15] The canal became the principal means of moving freight between New York City and the Great Lakes in that era. Thus did government subsidies provide necessary support for manufacturing. High school civics teachers and economics professors once drove home that history in their curriculum. And then in the 1950s and 1960s, when my generation became young adults, we lost sight of government's essential role in manufacturing just as globalization and the dismantling of trade barriers began to take their toll.

For family-owned textile manufacturers and their agents, like my father, the competition from abroad was disastrous. The few that survived managed to do so mainly through mergers with other manufacturers. In the process, those left standing in textiles brought the brokerage function in-house, selling directly to dyers or producers of finished goods. In a reduced industry, doing so made sense, although tens of thousands of people not officially counted as being employed in manufacturing, yet dependent upon it—like my father—lost their livelihoods. Fortunately, my father had retired before the role of independent broker ceased to exist, and his three sons had all by then elected other professions.

For a long stretch, through the 1960s and most of the 1970s, the mayhem in textile manufacturing, and among companies that turned textiles into clothing, bath towels, bedding, and other finished goods, overshadowed a somewhat more positive story elsewhere in U.S. manufacturing. Output continued to rise or hold steady in other sectors. And each year we continued to make significant quantities of steel, aluminum, aircraft, paper products, bicycles, motorcycles, tires, plastics, copper, refrigerators, kitchen stoves, eating utensils, electric motors, and much, much more. We still do, but starting in the 1950s, manufacturing output, which had long led growth in the national economy, fell behind, continuing to grow, but now more slowly, and in particular more slowly than such nonmanufacturing activities as real estate, finance, and Wall Street trading. It was as if U.S. manufacturing had climbed to the top of a hill only to slide most of the way back down. As the descent continued, the contribution made by manufacturing to GDP fell to just over 10 percent in the current decade from nearly 29 percent in the 1950s, according to the Department of Commerce Bureau of Economic Analysis, the scorekeeper in such matters. Simultaneously, the share of GDP (a broad measure of national income) from investment banking, Wall Street trading, insurance, and real estate transactions, the so-called financial sector of the economy, more than doubled, to 20 percent.[16]

As a consequence of this distortion, we pay less and less attention to the skills required to make things in factories, particularly on assembly lines, dismissing such work as routine and repetitive. Yet manufacturing labor is not more so than numerous tasks in the expanding financial and service sectors or in my profession, journalism. In my first newspaper job, for an afternoon newspaper in a small city, I had to produce five or six obituaries each morning, in time for a noon deadline, and I soon learned to fit a person's life story into a standard format. There was the opening paragraph announcing the death, the deceased's age, the cause of death, and one salient achievement in the person's life. The next two or three paragraphs elaborated on this and other biographical highlights, and the rest of the obit consisted of a chronological biography. There was skill involved, of course, in the quality of the writing and in the obit writer's ability to draw compelling information and anecdotes from family and friends, usually in telephone interviews. But the obituary's fixed structure simplified and speeded up the task, and it still does at most newspapers. Structured skill, I call this, and roughly similar structures turned out to be useful in writing up police and legislative developments and economics, my specialty, particularly the latest statistics. The same structured skill applies to factory work, but as manufacturing lost its status, we gradually forgot—if we ever really knew—that men and women on assembly lines have to acquire the skills needed to keep a line moving at a certain speed and with the fewest possible imperfections in the product being assembled on that line. We also forgot that assembly line workers often segue into more complex jobs as mechanics, shift managers, purchasing agents, electricians, foremen, engineers. The process requires continual training, with some line workers even taking leave from a factory to attend community colleges, their tuitions sometimes paid, at least in part, by their employer.

As a journalist, I finally visited enough factories and interviewed enough blue-collar workers to shake off the stereotype that white-collar office workers were more skilled than their blue-collar counterparts by virtue of working in offices rather than in factories. Factories house the same cross-section of restless, intelligent, achievement-oriented people as offices, where many of the tasks are also repetitive, requiring different but not necessarily superior skills. Covering economics for the *New York Times*, I soon realized that academics, faced with a shrinking manufacturing sector, had written it off as an important source of employment for skilled workers or as a generator of significant national income. They argued instead that the United States had "matured" into a finance-and-service-based economy, and that this was as good a source of growth and employment as manufacturing had been in an earlier era. What mattered, in their view, was economic growth and jobs, not the complexities involved in that growth. A dollar of national income generated by a restaurant or a law firm or a brokerage house became indistinguishable, according to the new prevailing wisdom, from a dollar earned in building an airliner or a computer or a car. Manufacturing had lost its way in the United States, and in the process millions of Americans—I would say *most* Americans—had been stripped of some of their status without realizing, or only vaguely realizing, what had happened to them.

I was one. Despite my father's work as a textile broker, the role played by manufacturing in shaping my own outlook and self-esteem—and indeed, my recognition that it had even played a role—did not dawn on me until the late 1960s, while I was out of the country, living in Buenos Aires and working as a foreign correspondent for the Associated Press. The Argentines had grown rich on beef and grain in the early decades of the twentieth century, and they yearned to grow rich again by emerging as the dominant manufacturing nation in Latin America, making for themselves more and more of the trappings of their middle-class lives instead of importing them from the United States. They tended to see manufacturing as essential to American identity, and Americans, including me, as having somehow incorporated sophisticated manufacturing know-how into our DNA. They spoke with me not just as a journalist or a friend, which many became in my six years in Argentina, but as a person who had been educated and shaped in the nation that was then, in the late 1960s, far and away the world's greatest source of manufactured goods. More than a few regretted that their grandparents or great-grandparents, emigrating from Europe, had gotten on what they described as the wrong boat, one that had taken them to Argentina, a primarily agricultural country, rather than to the United States, a superpower by virtue of its manufacturing achievements and its victory in World War II.

Two generations later, the wrong boat still rankled. The Argentines I got to know, or dealt with even casually, frequently explained to me that while they seemed like Argentines, they really were Italian or French or Spanish or British, preferring to identify with the industrialized European country from which their forebears had come. I ran into these assertions of identity most often in my dealings with taxicab drivers in Buenos Aires, a city with thousands of driver-owned cabs and a fare structure that made using cabs a not-too-expensive alternative to buses or subways. My accent pegged me as an American, and a few minutes into a ride, many of the drivers—the talkative ones, at least—found a way to steer even the most casual conversation onto the subject of nationality, with the goal of assuring me that while they were indeed Argentines, they weren't really Latin Americans; their parents or grandparents or great-grandparents were from one industrialized European country or another, just as mine were. While I embraced my American identity, not even imagining an alternative, they embraced their European roots, no matter how addicted many were to maté, the bitter-tasting Argentine tea that had originated among the gauchos.[17]

I realized that I had incorporated into my own identity America's huge success in manufacturing, a success then at its peak.[18] It set me and my wife apart, giving us a status that would begin to erode in our minds not long after we returned to the United States in the summer of 1973. We came home to a nation that took its huge success in manufacturing for granted, but not for much longer.

Three months after our return, the Arabs imposed their famous oil embargo, placing America's three largest auto manufacturers—General Motors, Ford, and Chrysler—in an untenable position. Overnight, the fuel-consuming vehicles that the Big Three insisted on manufacturing became much more expensive to drive than Japanese cars, which soon began to arrive in American ports by the hundreds of thousands. What's more, the Japanese cars were mechanically superior, breaking down less often, and in response we came to see the factory routines and practices that produced American cars as shoddy in comparison with those of the Japanese. For the first time, American manufacturers adopted Japanese practices, and the Japanese became the pacesetters for efficient factory production.

Consumer electronics followed a similar pattern. Although many such products were invented in the United States and initially made here, production gradually migrated to Japan and elsewhere in East Asia, which has become the manufacturing center not only of computers, cell phones, and numerous other electronic devices but of many everyday products that carry an American manufacturer's label—stoves, for example, or refrigerators, washing machines, microwave ovens, dryers, dishwashers, and motor scooters. The list is long and does not include the numerous products assembled in American factories with imported components, diluting the definition of "Made in America." On average, roughly 30 percent of the parts in any U.S.-manufactured product are imported.[19] The Eaton Corporation, to cite just one example, assembled truck transmissions at a factory in Cleveland, Ohio, but not all of the transmissions that Eaton sold in the United States. Some were imported from a factory in Brazil that Eaton owned.[20]

The United States, through such dilution, gradually squandered the huge lead in manufacturing that it possessed just after World War II. The war's devastation had left few factories undamaged in Western Europe and Asia, and the Soviet Union channeled its postwar efforts into reconstructing its own factories and those of the nations in its orbit. To compete effectively, the U.S. government provided subsidies that helped American manufacturers. The Marshall Plan was one such subsidy: it made $30 billion available to war-devastated nations, mostly in Europe, with the proviso that they spend the money in the United States to purchase the machinery and materials needed to rebuild their industries. As they rebuilt, our dominant position in manufacturing became all the greater. But that didn't last for long. Taking a cue from the Marshall Plan, many foreign manufacturers shifted to subsidies from their own governments. And those subsidies played a role in the decisions of American corporations to build factories abroad instead of increasing production in the United States.

GM, as everyone knows by now, is the beneficiary of huge subsidies from the federal government, including more than $10 billion just to bring the big multinational out of four years of bankruptcy in 2013. Despite this public support, GM manufactures more vehicles in its factories in China than any other auto company there, whether Chinese- or foreign-owned. Why not require that GM, in return for the federal bailout that saved it, make at least some of those cars in the United States and export them to China? The Chinese government would undoubtedly object; it subsidizes GM as well, after all. There would have to be a negotiated compromise, one that recognized an obligation on GM's part to expand production at home, given the life-saving subsidies it received from U.S. taxpayers.

That way of thinking does not exist yet. The subsidies in the United States that sustain domestic manufacturers are often used not to increase production but to move it around among cities and states. They are wielded as lures to persuade a manufacturer to locate a factory or a research center in one city rather than another. As a result of such wasteful intercity and interstate competition, GE in 2011, for example, decided to locate a second factory dedicated to manufacturing railroad locomotives in Fort Worth, Texas, rather than in Erie, Pennsylvania, next door to its first one—a loss for Erie, a gain for the winning city, and a zero-sum exercise for the entire nation. It was in fact worse than a zero-sum exercise, given the efficiencies that might have resulted from having the factories near each other.

My time in Argentina, in the late 1960s and early 1970s, coincided with that country's futile attempt to capture such efficiencies by becoming the manufacturing center for the Southern Cone and some adjacent countries: Brazil, Chile, Uruguay, Paraguay, Bolivia, and of course Argentina. That didn't happen. Brazil, with its much greater population and its larger nucleus of middle-income consumers, emerged as the region's manufacturing powerhouse, and the Argentines found themselves importing more and more from that country's factories. On a visit back to Buenos Aires in 1986, I found

Brazilian merchandise filling many store shelves and Portuguese gradually replacing English as the second language taught in secondary schools. One of my Argentine friends, staunchly pro-American in my days in Buenos Aires, now seemed less connected to the United States. He had represented American machinery manufacturers in their dealings with Argentina when I lived there, but by the mid-1980s he had shifted to representing mostly Brazilian machinery makers, traveling regularly to São Paulo to do so and no longer very often to New York.

Through most of my adult life American manufacturers were unchallenged in their supremacy. I had taken that for granted. We had manufactured not only the finished products but the nuts and bolts that held a car or a washing machine or a tractor together, as well as the copper and the wire and the steel and the aluminum and the textiles and the plastic used to make its parts. At our high point, in the mid-1950s, when manufacturers generated nearly 30 percent of GDP in the United States, their influence was enormous, and they hired thousands of the best college students. In those days, Charlie Wilson, the president of GM, was at the top of this heap, as well known to the public as Joe DiMaggio and widely quoted, particularly when he told Congress in 1953 that for years he had "thought that what was good for our country was good for General Motors, and vice versa."[21] He overstated the case, but not by a lot. If he had substituted *American manufacturers* for "General Motors"—embracing the entire sector instead of only its most emblematic company—the public would have agreed or taken no note of his comment.

I was an undergraduate at the University of Michigan in Ann Arbor, a stone's throw from Detroit, when Wilson made his famous public relations blunder. While I majored in English literature, many of my classmates focused on the sciences and engineering. Their principal tool in that pre-computer age was the slide rule; between classes, especially on a spring day, they walked across campus by the hundreds with the white, dagger-like calculators swinging gently from their belts, sometimes shining in the sunlight. These almost entirely male students were confident of the future, and with reason. Starting in early spring, recruiters from big manufacturing companies, particularly the auto giants, descended on campus and competed to hire graduating seniors, which they did by the dozens, and at respectable wages.

Foreign students also studied at Michigan in those years, and in growing numbers, but for the recruiters they did not yet have the cachet of their American counterparts. The goal of the foreign students was to return home and, in many cases, staff factories that American companies were opening overseas. These factories were not the cutting-edge foreign operations that many are today. They were instead extensions of operations in the United States, often using components and machinery imported from back home—so that rising output in a foreign factory automatically increased American domestic production as well. GM and Ford, for example, had big auto factories in Argentina during the years when I was the AP bureau chief there, from 1967 to 1973. The cars rolling off the Argentine assembly lines, however, were adaptations of models that had been designed and produced for American consumers. What's more, the American-made machinery on those Argentine assembly lines was often secondhand, having been used first by Ford or GM or Chrysler in their U.S. factories and then shipped abroad. We did not yet think of the Big Three auto giants as multinationals. They were instead American manufacturers with subsidiary operations abroad, spinning off versions of American models three or four years after they had first appeared in the United States.

Sophisticated parts, such as carburetors, were shipped from U.S. factories. Even most of the steel in the cars that GM and Ford made in Argentina came from America—a point that a visiting U.S. Steel Company executive proudly, and arrogantly, made clear to me and to other journalists during a press briefing in Buenos Aires. Only in the mid-1970s did an Argentine consortium finally open a major steel mill within the country, in incipient defiance of American dominance.

More than a generation later, auto assembly lines are disappearing from Argentina. They are concentrated instead in Brazil to serve that country's huge domestic market and also those of Brazil's neighbors, including Argentina. The same big international companies that made cars in South America in my day still make them now. But the cars they produce are no longer spinoffs. They are in many cases designed in Brazil. The steel that goes into them is manufactured there and in neighboring, less populous countries, again including Argentina. Ditto for other components. Many of the vehicles themselves run not on gasoline, as their American cousins do, but on diesel oil or propane, which means the motors are different. Modern multinationals, in other words, make in Latin America cars designed for that market, and do so in manufacturing operations that are increasingly parallel to those in the United States, rather than extensions of them. No wonder, then, that U.S. manufacturing grows more slowly than it once did, and in fact more slowly than other significant sectors of the economy.

The shift became noticeable in the final decade of the twentieth century, with the realization that Asia and Europe were rivaling the United States as giant consumer markets, and factories in those countries had to be on par with those in America. Consumer spending in China or the European Union might not yet be equal to that of the United States, but it has been growing more rapidly, as has factory output, with large chunks of that growth accounted for by factories owned by multinationals. What draws them is not just the growing number of customers with middle-class incomes, but the subsidies offered by governments to defray the cost and, in effect, bulk up profit—or even make profit possible in the first place. As a nation, we Americans do ourselves a disservice in failing to acknowledge these facts of life.

The multinationals are more realistic. Given the steady growth of consumer spending in China, India, or the European Union, big multinationals such as GM, Dow Chemical, GE, and IBM have opened factories in these countries—in Dow's case a dozen in China alone, plus a sophisticated research center near Shanghai. Explaining this strategy during an interview in 2011 at Dow's headquarters in Midland, Michigan, Andrew N. Liveris, then Dow's chairman, told me that "overseas," and in particular China, "I get tax incentives, and I get incentives to go to certain locations where they offer us utilities, infrastructure, and land. I get access to human capital. I get all sorts of support to help train that human capital."[22] In exchange, Dow made in China such products as refrigerator insulation, a foamy petrochemical that might have been exported to China from a Dow factory in America. Barack Obama—or George W. Bush before him—could have insisted that this be done as part of a federal industrial policy whose goal was to increase factory output in the United States.

In the early years of such "offshoring," the public outcry was considerable. It died away, however, as manufacturing's share of output and employment within the United States continued to fall. Unable to stop the process, the public in effect acquiesced, and so did the administration, although Obama, at the outset of his presidency in 2009, appointed a task force to report on ways to revive manufacturing. But the committee dissolved as its members resigned and were not replaced.[23] We had finally acquiesced to the argument—after having had it drilled into us for years—that the service sector, the financial sector, and "advanced manufacturing" were more suitable ways to make a living in the United States than old-style factory production. Donald Trump's presidency may put a dent in that way of thinking. If so, it was a long time coming.

Since 1989, we have been closing factory buildings right and left, leaving more than forty thousand facilities vacant or idle.[24] Some have been converted to warehouses or even Walmart-size retail stores, but the majority remain standing, unused and shuttered, particularly in urban areas, as anyone can see riding an Amtrak passenger train between Baltimore and New York or a municipal bus whose scheduled route takes its passengers from the central business district of many cities in the eastern United States out to the city line. The Federal Reserve reports on the empty factories in a bland statistic published every quarter, and we essentially ignore it. The bland statistic is the "capacity utilization rate," which summarizes how much factory floor space is in use across the nation and also the rate or speed at which the machinery is being run. If all of a factory's floor space is in use, and the people occupying that space are running the machinery at a steady pace while working diligently themselves, then the capacity utilization rate is 100 percent. Eighty percent or more would signal a booming industrial sector, as in the good old days. According to the Federal Reserve, which collects this data, American manufacturers used around 75 percent of their production capacity in 2016, down from annual estimates of more than 80 percent through most of the 1980s and 1990s.[25]

Multinational corporations have accounted for much of that decline, by moving production abroad to supply overseas markets rather than exporting from the United States, and to lower the cost of manufacturing merchandise for American consumers. As the exodus continued and work disappeared, the bargaining power of American factory workers plummeted, and many of the skills that keep a factory running were devalued. By the late 1990s the truly multinational manufacturer—headquartered in the United States and running sophisticated factories spread across the globe—had come fully to life.

2

Redefining Skill

For more than a generation now, we have accepted the distorted proposition that the truly skilled have college educations, while manual skills constitute a lower order. By that standard, manufacturers in the United States should concentrate on producing only the most sophisticated products—for example, jet aircraft, rocket engines, space satellites, intricate medical devices—and the workers producing these complex products, even many on assembly lines, should have college degrees. According to this strange (yet standard) way of thinking, we should no longer want to manufacture everyday merchandise—for example, the clothes we wear, the appliances in our kitchens, the computers in our homes and offices, the cell phones in our pockets, the watches on our wrists, the toys in children's playrooms, the silverware on our dinner tables, the metal frames that hold our family photos, the lightbulbs in our homes, the spark plugs in our cars, the faucet handles in our bathrooms.

In fact, our conventional view of the labor that goes into manufacturing overlooks quite basic facts about the nature of assembly line work. Not infrequently assembly line workers performing repetitive tasks get to know the machines they operate well enough to perform minor repairs without having to call in a mechanic. Some also suggest ways to do their jobs more efficiently or less expensively. In the 1980s and 1990s, factory managers hailed these contributions from the rank and file and even invited reporters, including me, to sit in on meetings of assembly line workers and supervisors where the former suggested ways to improve the production process, and the latter pledged that if any of the suggestions displaced workers, they would be transferred to vacancies elsewhere in the factory without cuts in pay. These "quality circles," as they were sometimes called, accepted as a given the skills inherent in repetitive manual labor. We recognize, of course, the skills possessed by some manual workers, such as machinists, welders, carpenters, plumbers, electricians, steamfitters, upholsterers, and bricklayers. We seek a skilled electrician to install new wiring in our homes, a skilled upholsterer to re-cover a living room couch, a skilled plumber to repair a leaky sink, a skilled mason to construct the walls of a brick house, or a skilled helmsman to keep our riverboat from running aground—a skill that Samuel Clemens, later to become famous as Mark Twain, struggled to acquire in an early job as a cub pilot on a Mississippi River paddle wheeler. Years later, in *Life on the Mississippi*, he recounted the experience and his surprise that steering a boat down a wide river in broad daylight would require so much seat-of-the-pants knowledge of the river's numerous sandbars and treacherous currents.[1] What we don't acknowledge is the skill inherent in virtually all manual labor, including assembly line work. Even sympathetic supervisors—as well as the workers themselves—may fail to recognize the skills frequently on display on assembly lines. It is in the often graceful, efficient ways in which workers move their bodies as they swing a car door into place along an auto assembly line, for example, or stack finished tires at a Goodyear factory.

Two reasons for this bias stand out. One is that a disproportionately large number of African Americans and Latinos are engaged in manual work in the United States, and anti-black and anti-Hispanic sentiment demeans the manual skills in which so many have come to excel. The sociologist Richard Sennett put this bluntly: "As we withdrew from being a nation that honored skilled manual labor domestically, we left this work mainly to immigrants and to blacks, and that reinforced the sense that this is not real American work."[2] The other major reason behind the bias is the use of a bachelor's degree as a sorting mechanism. Much more in recent years than in the past, the degree serves as a signal—often false—that its bearers are skilled, and therefore more deserving of a job than less-educated men and women. They may not possess a specific skill on graduation day, but they possess the mental discipline, intelligence, and book knowledge that make the act of learning a new skill—which is itself a worthwhile skill—easier and faster.

In the summer of 1954, just a few weeks after earning a BA from the University of Michigan, I returned to my parents' home in New York, where I took a job as a buyer's assistant for Kobacker Stores, a small family-owned chain of Midwestern department stores.[3] While the stores themselves were located mostly in midsize Ohio cities, the fifteen or so buyers and their assistants worked out of a New York office. Except for me, none had graduated from college or had attended one full-time, although two of the assistants were taking night courses at the City College of New York, hoping to become licensed accountants. Neither they nor anyone else in the office, however, considered formal education beyond high school necessary to do their current jobs well, although the work was in fact intellectually demanding.

For example, the buyers of men's sports shirts and of women's skirts placed orders in October for the merchandise that would be sold the following spring and early summer. They had to anticipate the styles that would be popular, the prices the stores could charge, the quantities likely to be sold, quality, delivery dates, shipping, and warehouse costs. Juggling these and other variables, the buyers were, in sum, very skilled at a complex job from which they would have been excluded sixty years later for lack of a bachelor's degree. Having one in the mid-1950s made me a novelty, and also a puzzle. Others in the office asked me why I would waste a college education on their trade. It made them uneasy, and I found myself explaining, defensively, that I had taken the job as a stopgap until I could land work as a newspaper reporter. I eventually did so, entering a profession that is intellectually demanding and skilled, but not more so than buying merchandise for a department store chain.

Like department store buyers and assistant buyers, newspaper reporters and editors today are almost always graduates of a four-year college. That was not the case when I left Kobacker to become a reporter, first at the *Daily Argus* in Mount Vernon, New York, and two years later at the Associated Press. In those days, half my colleagues at the Argus and a smaller percentage at the AP had not gone past high school or had dropped out of college after a year or two. That was also the pattern in the hierarchy at manufacturing companies: more than a few chief executives had started in stockrooms or on assembly lines after high school and had risen over the years, acquiring their skills on the job.[4]

The G.I. Bill after World War II amplified college as a source of skill.[5] With the federal government paying tuition and living expenses, millions of veterans who would not have attended college before the war earned bachelor's degrees and then took jobs that, before the war, would not have required a college education. The Korean War reinforced this trend, making a new surge of veterans eligible for the G.I. Bill and the college education it subsidized. By the early 1960s, a bachelor's degree had become a signal that the possessor was more likely than a high school graduate to pick up the skills that a particular job required. That signal had long existed. But with far fewer college graduates available, employers accepted a high school diploma as evidence of schooling sufficient for work that, just a few years later, required a college degree. By then, the G.I. Bill had made a college education more affordable than it had been in the past, flooding the nation with college grads and devaluing the capabilities of those with only high school diplomas.

My parents insisted that I go to college and, after four years, return home with a bachelor's degree. If I had wanted to study engineering, or take courses to qualify me for medical or law school, that would have been fine in their eyes. If, on the other hand, I had wanted to major in English literature or history or philosophy or foreign languages, that would also have been fine—just so long as I earned that bachelor's degree, a necessary emblem of belonging to the middle class. As for earning a living, I could learn how to do that later, on the job, like so many had done in my parents' generation. I took their advice, majoring in English literature with a minor in philosophy, two fields that came with plenty of essay assignments. In hindsight, those three-to-five page essays were effective training in concise writing, a necessary skill in journalism.

Still, many of my older colleagues at the *Daily Argus* and the AP wrote effectively, although their educations had ended with high school. As they aged and retired in the late twentieth century, however, their replacements were almost always college educated, thanks to the huge pool of college graduates that the G.I. Bill made possible.

Given the surge of workers holding college degrees, those with only high school diplomas—still the great majority of the men and women on factory assembly lines—came to be seen as underachievers, which meant that manufacturers encountered less and less censure when they closed domestic factories and in many cases moved production abroad, laying off millions of high school–educated blue-collar workers.[6] As the layoffs spread beyond manufacturing, involving college-educated workers as well, the public gradually acquiesced. In the case of manufacturing workers, we eliminated 60 percent of their jobs in a single generation, nullifying their skills in making factories function. Those who remained found themselves staffing increasingly automated assembly lines that nonetheless required roughly the same manual skills as the old lines, only now the survivors reprogrammed computer-operated machinery, a task more or less equivalent to the repairs and adjustments that line workers have always made.

Skill among assembly line workers is a recurrent issue. In the early twentieth century, Henry Ford famously paid his employees on the nation's first assembly line five dollars a day, a wage high enough to lure craftsmen skilled in building cars by hand into building them instead on a moving line, with each of the workers stationed along that line performing a discrete task, requiring a fraction of the worker's full complement of skills. Ford paid workers well, in effect, to suppress their array of skills.[7] And his contemporary Frederick Taylor, in his classic study *The Principles of Scientific Management*, codified this skills suppression, encouraging the practice on a grand scale. He did so by breaking down the manufacture of a complex product into hundreds of separate tasks, each one performed with a minimum of skill along a moving assembly line. Workers in general accepted the trade-off: good wages in exchange for suppressed skills, and that has continued into the twenty-first century.[8]

Nonetheless, more than a few assembly line workers have continued to maintain and even enhance their skills on their own. The Strong brothers, Mark and Tim, were working on the assembly line at a General Motors factory in Lansing, Michigan, when I encountered them in 2009—not at the factory but at their own small machine shop in a rented building near their homes. In their off-hours, they operated as outside contractors, making special tools that GM purchased to use in the repair and maintenance of giant presses at the Lansing plant, which stamped sheets of steel into fenders, doors, and hoods. After a cutback in auto production in the fall of 2008, the Strong brothers found themselves still employed full-time on the assembly line, thanks to their seniority, but GM was purchasing fewer of their tools. So they turned in their off-hours to what had been until then a minor activity: machining wing spars by day in their shop for the A10 Thunderbolt, an Air Force fighter jet, while continuing to work the night shift at the GM plant, performing the repetitive tasks that make factories efficient but make less use of the skills that factory workers so often possess.[9]

The evidence of skill is subtle. Walk through a factory parking lot during a shift and count the pickup trucks with large toolboxes embedded behind the cabs, each indicating that the driver is a skilled manual worker who uses those tools in his off-hours. In a late 1990s study of blue-collar workers at a (now closed) GM plant in Linden, New Jersey, the sociologist Ruth Milkman found that many line workers undertook home renovations and other skilled work in their spare time. "I have often thought," Milkman said, "that these extracurricular jobs were an effort on the part of the workers to regain their dignity after suffering the degradation of repetitive assembly line work in the factory."[10] But degradation wasn't the only problem. Modernization also played a role, by cutting back the number of people needed, and in doing so, creating a pool of seasoned yet unemployed production workers. In the steel industry, for example, the so-called mini-mills that emerged in the 1980s—companies such as Steel Dynamics in Fort Wayne, Indiana—reduced production costs by more than 50 percent compared to traditional mills like those operated by U.S. Steel. Or so Keith E. Busse, the chairman of Steel Dynamics, insisted when I visited his mini-mill in the fall of 2012. Busse's company, and others like it, cut costs in part through innovations in their supply chain and production process. They saved on the cost of raw material by using scrap steel mixed with iron ore, which is less expensive than pure ore, and they replaced blast furnaces with electric arc furnaces, which are more fuel efficient. Moreover, crucially, they cut their labor costs: Steel Dynamics used fewer workers per ton of steel than such big companies as Bethlehem Steel or U.S. Steel.

For similar reasons, the number of people employed in the entire manufacturing sector, not only in steel, has steadily fallen over the past thirty-five years. The shrinking of manufacturing employment has created a "skills surplus"—a surplus of people skilled in the numerous tasks that keep a factory running, from assembly line workers on up. One of the effects of a skills *surplus* is that it leads to a general decline in status for *all* workers. For example, factory owners once employed tens of thousands of mechanics skilled in maintaining and repairing machinery. They wanted them on the payroll, fearful that enough mechanics wouldn't be available for quick repair when a machine broke down, halting an assembly line. A skills surplus, on the other hand, means that machinery mechanics are, in effect, standing by, off the payroll but available for a repair job on short notice. They are often called in not individually by a particular factory that needs their services, but by a third party such as Advanced Technology Services (ATS), which contracts with factory owners to service their machinery, sending in mechanics as needed to repair and maintain machines that mold parts, for example, or braid strands of copper wire into cables, or heat and shape metal, or keep a conveyor belt moving or repair and maintain the robots stationed along modern assembly lines. Skilled people must do this work, but they increasingly do so on the rosters of companies like Advanced Technology Services, which employs 2,500 mechanics, with the understanding that when work slows, the mechanics agree to reassignment at other factories or to unpaid furloughs.[11]

Ask the ATS leadership if America suffers from a skills shortage and the answer from Donald K. Johnson, a vice president, is no.[12] For example, when an Eaton Corporation or an A.O. Smith decides to outsource the maintenance of machinery in their factories, Johnson explains, "We hire some of their own workers"—mainly those, ironically, who face layoffs because of the manufacturer's decision to outsource maintenance. ATS also sends in technicians already on its staff, renting them to customers, sometimes for months. About 25 percent of the ATS technicians are recruited from what Johnson described as the huge pool of men and women who have been trained as mechanics in the armed forces and seek to make use of their training after leaving the service.[13] "They have the skills we need and the military has also taught them how to work," Johnson explained.[14] The armed forces, then, provide one steady source of trained mechanics; layoffs and cutbacks, another. Indeed, after thirty years of steadily declining employment in manufacturing, the abundance of men and women skilled in machinery repair gives personnel managers the luxury of renting workers instead of hiring them. Why hire, and in doing so take on the numerous obligations of being an employer—including the funding of pensions and health insurance, vacation pay and severance—when you can rent skilled workers as you need them from the huge pool of people that an ATS has accumulated? Its customers in the second decade of the twenty-first century have included giant manufacturers such as Caterpillar, A.O. Smith, Textron, Honda, and GM. Under the cover of a skills *shortage*—when there is in fact a skills *surplus*—these iconic corporations, and many others not so iconic, have rented skilled mechanics at less than the cost of hiring and training them.

ATS began as a subsidiary of Caterpillar, the heavy-equipment manufacturer headquartered in Peoria, Illinois, where ATS also has its headquarters. Caterpillar in the 1980s saw an opportunity to leverage its skilled mechanics by renting them to other manufacturers when they weren't needed at Caterpillar. Then, in 1996, a group of mechanics staffing the rental operation formed ATS and signed up Caterpillar as the first customer. Two decades later, ATS supplies teams of skilled mechanics to a hundred or more manufacturers, often for weeks at a time. On the job, they are indistinguishable from a factory's own employees except for their hourly pay (sometimes less) and a red-and-white identity patch sewn over the breast pockets of their work shirts. "We are the maintenance departments for those factories," Jeffrey Owens, president of ATS, explained.[15]

One of the ATS clients that I visited, in the fall of 2014, was World's Finest Chocolate, a family-owned candy manufacturer, more than sixty years old, whose sole factory is located near Chicago O'Hare International Airport. In 2012, the Opler family employed about thirty people (one-seventh of its staff) in machinery maintenance. Twenty-seven of these mechanics became ATS employees that year when ATS took over the factory's maintenance (the rest retired). Once the twenty-seven mechanics had made the shift, they found themselves working for Heather Betts, a young mechanical engineer on the ATS staff brought to Chicago as the site manager at the chocolate factory. She insisted to me that the mechanics were better off because, as ATS employees, they could look forward to careers and promotions at a company that valued their skills more than the managers of World's Finest Chocolate had. That may have been the case, but in accepting the move to ATS, the mechanics lowered the odds that the two hundred or so assembly line workers they had left behind would have the leverage to organize a union and then bargain for higher wages and job security. While still on staff, the mechanics were in a position to support the assembly line workers by striking if the latter did, or by not striking but engaging in a work slowdown—dragging out repairs— if the company brought in outsiders to replace the assembly line workers. Without willing mechanics, a machinery breakdown can halt an assembly line in any factory and even shut it down. The Oplers understood this. "In our negotiations with ATS we specified that having skilled mechanics available on all shifts and at all times was the reason for going with that company," Edmund F. Opler, the chocolate company's chief executive, explained to me during an interview in his office.[16] "We found that we could hold ATS to a higher standard than we were able to attain on our own."[17]

No wonder ATS grew from a single client, Caterpillar, to a company with more than a hundred corporate clients twenty-five years later.[18] Among ATS's customers and other manufacturers like them, the phrase *skills shortage* is code for sidestepping unions. And indeed, only 10 percent of America's manufacturing workers belonged to unions in 2015, down from 15.6 percent in 2000, according to the Bureau of Labor Statistics.[19] Another ATS customer is Milwaukee Gear, which manufactures ratchet wheels in various diameters for use in engines and machinery and employed 250 people in 2016, most of them machinists. Years ago, when manufacturing contributed much more to the national income, especially in industrial cities such as Milwaukee, machinists and mechanics were easier to come by. "Even ten years ago, we could hire them away from another company, but no more," Azmi Issa, Milwaukee Gear's plant manager, told me.[20] "In today's world, once a good machinist or mechanic has a job, he keeps it. The pool of people willing to jump from job to job, confident that their skills are in demand, is just about gone. Their skills *are* in demand, but in their minds the risk of falling into unemployment is too great."

So Issa turned to ATS, which sent in nine people skilled in machining and in the maintenance of machining equipment. That was in 2010, and half a decade later ATS employees were still on-site, training younger people newly hired by Milwaukee Gear and also doing some of the maintenance work themselves while the new hires gained enough experience to pull their weight. In a factory environment, graduates of vocational high schools usually get up to speed more quickly than others, but Milwaukee, like the nation as a whole, does not have as many vocational high schools as it once did, and apprenticeship programs in manufacturing have similarly dwindled. So ATS steps in, filling the gap (or attempting to do so), while public school systems in the United States have focused more and more on history, English, mathematics, sciences, and other standard subjects more likely to prepare young people for college than for manual work.

It's an explanation that gets twisted in the telling. According to many academics, policy makers, politicians, journalists, and even some union leaders, there aren't more factories because there aren't enough workers with the right skills to man them. In his State of the Union address in January 2012, President Obama told Americans that he hears "from many business leaders who want to hire in the United States but can't find workers with the right skills . . . think about that—openings at a time when millions of Americans are looking for work."[21] In his State of the Union address two years later, Obama was a bit more charitable, calling for more apprenticeship programs to train newly hired young people on the job and thus reduce the shortage of skilled workers.[22]

If there were truly a skills shortage, factory owners would cut back production or cancel second or third shifts for lack of qualified workers. I have visited numerous manufacturers over the past decade and have yet to find that happening. When manufacturers bemoan a lack of skilled people readily available for hiring, more often than not they mean a lack of job candidates who are already skilled enough to go right to work with no more than a few days of training. Such an insistence on being able to hire fully trained workers was not standard practice in the United States until the late twentieth century. Apprenticeship programs, on-the-job learning, veterans teaching newcomers, and probationary employment for three or four months were standard procedures for nurturing skill—and most likely would still be in use if the pool of people seeking work weren't so large, passing the 25 million mark in 2015.[23] If that number were to shrink, the emphasis on hiring those who are already skilled would diminish, along with much of the talk about skills shortages. Needing workers, companies would hire and train the unemployed, as they have in the past, instead of shunning them, claiming they are unemployable because they lack the necessary skills.

In good times, when employers seek out and compete for workers, the phrase *skills shortage*—and the insult embedded in it—disappears from the public conversation. That was the case for thirty years after World War II, when the unemployed were a smaller share of the population and companies hunted for workers, training those they could find, not only in manual skills but also in skills up and down the spectrum. A young attorney just out of law school would be snapped up by a law firm, and then spend a first year drafting contracts and assisting experienced lawyers, or a young engineer would join a construction company after graduating and start out drafting blueprints. As new college graduates, they lacked the professional skills that experience would bring them, but no one held them up as examples of a skills shortage. The new hires' employers felt lucky to have recruited them at a time when there were not enough young lawyers and engineers to meet their needs, and the firms that won out in this hiring race "solved" any skills shortage by completing the recruits' training themselves. Similarly, home builders in a booming construction market vied to hire carpenters and plumbers when there weren't enough already licensed as professionals in these fields and certainly not enough rookies in the pipeline seeking experience en route to getting licensed. In that sense there *was* a skills shortage, but one tied to the low unemployment rate and the scarcity of people available for training. Which is why, one summer while I was still in high school, I managed to get work as a plumber's assistant on a construction site.

The first week on the job, my boss assigned me to dig a trench four or five feet deep and three or four feet across to bring underground pipes from the street into a nearly finished home, a distance of about forty feet. This was in the days before tractor-like excavators regularly performed such seemingly unskilled tasks. I had the physical strength to dig the trench but not the stamina to complete the work in the allotted four to five hours; nor did I have the skill to keep the sides perpendicular without their collapsing. In the end, I stood by while an experienced ditch digger completed the job. Watching him, I admired his stamina, strength, and, yes, skill— and thought of college as an escape into physically easier, not into higher-skilled, work.

Ditch digging with a shovel gave way, of course, to motorized excavators. We tend to think of an excavator operator as more skilled than a ditch digger or an assembly line worker, but in doing so we ignore the fact that skills can't, or shouldn't, be placed in a hierarchy if each produces a necessary or valuable result. Yet that is what we do, locking ourselves into a definition of skills that grades them subjectively and, in doing so, helps to justify, in the case of manufacturing, the outsourcing to other countries of "low-skilled" or "un-skilled" work.

People ask me if manufacturing is coming back to America. They ask partly to be polite, to show some interest in a subject that obviously absorbs me. But many are also uneasy that so many of the products on which they depend are made overseas. American consumers acquiesced to this inflow more than thirty years ago, accepting the proposition that "low-end" manufacturing had become the domain of less skilled, less expensive workers in countries not yet as highly industrialized as the United States. Let them have the work, our economists and policymakers argued. Americans should focus on making sophisticated products that require their superior skills, particularly the skills attached to a four-year college degree.[24] With the portion of the population holding four-year degrees at only around 30 percent, and not rising all that fast, we have come to see ourselves as a nation afflicted with a skills shortage. Increase the share of college graduates, we tell ourselves, and in doing so we will diminish this shortage. Economic activity will accelerate, and manufacturers will forge ahead right here in America, not in the output of low-end merchandise, but through "advanced manufacturing."

That is a shamelessly exclusionary definition of skill, given the high cost of a college education, the relatively small share of the population that has one, and society's need for any number of skills that we arbitrarily categorize as "low end." Picture the United States without efficient garbage collectors (yes, their job requires skill); parking lot attendants nimbly and quickly manipulating cars in a busy, overcrowded lot (without denting fenders); waiters and waitresses with enough dexterity and experience to take dinner orders accurately, and then agilely carry from the kitchen half a dozen

plates of food on an overcrowded tray; or factory workers partici-
pating in the assembly of a complex product while it moves by them
at a steady pace. Ignoring the variety and complexity of skills de-
manded by the labor market, we veer more than ever in the direc-
tion of college as the breeding ground for those skills that count.[25]
And in the name of this new standard, we have closed hundreds
of vocational high schools where teenagers once received initial
training en route to becoming auto and aircraft mechanics, electricians, welders, carpenters, pipefitters, masons, plumbers, tool-
and-die makers, cooks, waiters, tailors, and assembly line workers.
Vocational high schools got young people started on plumbing and
other trades, and they prepared many graduates for factory jobs
and for advancement up a factory's hierarchy. The plumber I
worked for graduated from a vocational high school in the 1940s
and did not go the factory route. But others did, and he could have.
He was an even-tempered, articulate man, with a decisive person-
ality, and to this day I imagine that if he had taken a job on a factory assembly line, he would eventually have risen to be a corporate
executive, sans a BA or an MBA degree.

A generation later, the same vocational education route no longer existed. As factory jobs disappeared in a precipitous decline after
1979, so did vocational training and the opportunities it fostered.
Cincinnati, for example, had five vocational high schools when I first
visited there in the 1980s, on assignment for the *New York Times*.
These high schools had been publicly funded for years as an alternative to academic high schools. They prepared hundreds of young
people for blue-collar jobs in the Cincinnati area, once a quintes-
sentially industrial city on the Ohio River where Procter & Gamble
and General Electric, among others, had huge factory complexes.[26]

All five schools are gone today, their funding gradually eliminated as school boards in many districts nationwide have held down costs. The manufacturing companies that drew employees from these high schools might have pushed to keep them open, but like manufacturers everywhere in America, those in Cincinnati employed fewer and fewer people—and they gradually ceased to rely upon the vocational high schools as a source of new hires. As the schools closed, thousands of teenagers found themselves funneled into Cincinnati's surviving, college-oriented high schools. Many had no intention of going to college, and some dropped out of school short of graduation. More recently, some have endured a long bus ride to a regional vocational high school that was eventually opened on the outskirts of the city.

Foreseeing this unwinding, ministers of churches with black congregations—in a city whose population was two-thirds African American in the late twentieth century—campaigned unsuccessfully to keep at least some of the vocational schools open within the city. As the ministers saw it, many dropouts in their congregations would have graduated from a nearby vocational high school. They would have had more interest in coursework that prepared them for manual trades than in courses that steered students toward college. When I asked various Cincinnati officials about the concerns of the black ministers, they pointed out that community colleges were replacing public high schools in providing vocational training. But community colleges charge tuition, unlike vocational high schools, and they require a high school diploma for entry—an obvious irony. No wonder the high school dropout rate in Cincinnati reached 50 percent of the student body in some recent years. As Ron D. Wright, a former president of Cincinnati State Technical and

Community College, once told me, "Without vocational training in the public schools, we will have unskilled people destined for poverty."[27] His college was housed in a graceful brick building that once had been a public vocational high school.

What happened in Cincinnati has happened, to one degree or another, across the nation as property owners have resisted increases in real estate taxes, the major source of funding for public schools. Closing vocational high schools or cutting back their programs was politically easier to effect in a country that had degraded the value of manual skills. In addition, closing vocational high schools often produced more savings than closing academic high schools would have, in part by no longer having to outfit workshops with lathes, power saws, drill presses, welding irons, and numerous other expensive tools, not to mention autos and even small aircraft, which students at some vocational high schools were taught to dismantle and reassemble as a routine part of their coursework. In particular, courses that prepared teenagers for jobs in manufacturing were eliminated at a greater rate between 1990 and 2009 than courses focused on other occupations, such as repair and transportation, according to data furnished by the National Association of State Directors of the Career Technical Education Consortium.

In some cases, vocational training has become part of the curriculum at new regional high schools supported jointly by several school districts. They are schools focused mainly on developing their students' manual skills while also preparing graduates for enrollment in a four-year college. Eagle Tech Academy, which opened in the fall of 2011 in Columbia City, Indiana, is such a hybrid. Its goal is to meld academic and vocational training and in doing so send its graduates on to a four-year college, if that is their preference, or into skilled trades and factory employment, the route taken by most of the students. I toured the school a year after it opened. Forty percent of its five hundred students had been recruited from the academic high school in Columbia City, with the rest coming from school districts nearby. At Eagle Tech, students take academic courses such as English, science, and mathematics in their freshman and sophomore years; after that, the curriculum swings mainly toward preparation for the skilled trades: electrician, plumber, machinist, auto mechanic, welder. Students who decide midway through Eagle Tech that they want to go on to college have the option of shifting back to Columbia City's academic high school, or they may stay on at Eagle Tech and still apply to college.

The school's principal, Braden "Brady" Mullett, a former high school science teacher, said the aim of the Eagle Tech curriculum is to "create relevance." He explained *relevance* by describing a staple in the curriculum, in which students are assigned to read the John Steinbeck classic *Of Mice and Men* and then do a "project" on the Great Depression, the period in which the novel is set. "We still discuss writing style and Steinbeck's place among the writers of his day," Mullett explained. "But that is not the emphasis. The emphasis is on what life was like then. We do literature and history like any high school, but the two subjects are taught together, not as separate courses."[28] That helps to compress the academic course work so that sufficient time can be devoted to vocational training. Put another way, vocational and academic training are packed into eight high school semesters, and the students are encouraged to work together, even to form teams to help one another absorb all the material. Such teamwork encourages, indeed demands, collaboration—a vital skill for nearly all factory-based jobs.

These experiments in vocational education, while important, are only part of a larger solution. In U.S. manufacturing, employment in the summer of 2016 had fallen to the same level as in the summer of 1941, just months before the outbreak of World War II, according to the Bureau of Labor Statistics.[29] The jobs are not out there and won't be as long as U.S.-headquartered multinational corporations continue to dominate manufacturing, churning out 66 percent of what is made in the country but nevertheless preferring to manufacture offshore a significant share of what they sell at home. In short, the absence of a skilled workforce is not an obstacle to more manufacturing in the United States: the obstacles lie elsewhere.

3

Urban Manufacturing

The first thing you learn about manufacturing in St. Louis—or in Detroit or Buffalo or Cleveland or Chicago or Baltimore, for that matter—is that multistory factory buildings are not suited for modern manufacturing. With their high ceilings and big windows, these solid brick structures, which had flourished as urban factories through most of the twentieth century, make lovely loft apartment buildings in the twenty-first century, and more than a few have been converted into residences, certainly in St. Louis. A Ford Motor Company assembly plant and a Falstaff brewery, for example, are now attractive condominiums.[1] Some former factories have become warehouses, which is useful in a crossroads city. In St. Louis the crossroads are the Mississippi River, carrying cargo north and south, and the Missouri River, going west, together with the numerous highways and railroad freight lines that hook up with these rivers. But the supply of potential warehouses far exceeds the demand in this age of rapid delivery, and many such buildings are empty and sometimes even sealed, their windows painted over and opaque. Others have been torn down and the huge tracts on which they stood have become acres of grassy scrubland, often next door to crumbling residential neighborhoods where erstwhile factory workers once lived and still occasionally do. Their former employers have plainly given up on urban manufacturing, sometimes moving overseas but almost always away from U.S. cities in pursuit of more land on which to put a modern factory building, which is a different creature.

The modern factory often resembles a well-lighted, high-ceilinged aircraft hangar: a single-story structure spacious enough to house one or more jet airliners simultaneously, but housing instead a machinery-intensive assembly line snaking its way along a thick concrete floor. Some manufacturers have made the transition without leaving St. Louis, often getting the municipal government to subsidize larger quarters in urban neighborhoods, in buildings that otherwise would be shuttered.

The Wunderlich Fibre Box Company—family owned for five generations—is one of these subsidized neighborhood factories. The Wunderlichs make corrugated fiberboard containers, similar to thick cardboard, on Clinton Street in north St. Louis, in a building they remodeled after the municipal government purchased the property and resold it to them at a discount to assure their continued presence as proprietors of a functioning urban manufacturing company. The newer factory is just across the street from the family's old quarters, a two-story structure converted by the company into a facility for equipment maintenance (on the ground floor) and office space (upstairs). The office staff includes artists and designers who customize the containers for some clients, designing corporate logos, for example, to be printed on the fiberboard, or on display shelves fashioned from fiberboard. These too are made in the factory across the street.

Corrugated boxes of various sizes, folded flat for easier shipping and for compact storage, are delivered in quantity to numerous purchasers, who assemble them as needed to pack and ship their products. In 1860, when the Wunderlichs started up in St. Louis, the first containers they made were wooden barrels, which were easy for a customer to nail shut and roll down a loading ramp onto a steamship plying the Mississippi or moving west along the Missouri. By the late 1800s, more than fifty riverboats a day loaded or unloaded barrels in St. Louis. The barrels eventually gave way to more efficient containers, and the Wunderlichs shifted with the times, even renaming the company periodically to reflect more up-to-date technology.[2] Transportation also changed, and the city eventually deeded to the company the street outside the factory so that tractor-trailers could be backed up to shipping bays and loaded or unloaded more efficiently. Without ample room to maneuver big trucks, many manufacturers today cannot easily locate in urban neighborhoods.

All this Robert A. Wunderlich, the fifth-generation family chieftain, explained to me as we walked through his factory and out onto Clinton Street.[3] He never uses the phrase *industrial policy* in describing the city's essential role in preserving Wunderlich as an urban manufacturer. "The city acquired the property for the new factory and then sold it to us for a reasonable amount," he said, making clear that the reasonable amount was significantly less than what the city had paid.[4] In addition, the city funneled $200,000 in cash to the Wunderlichs from a development fund set aside for this purpose to finance the land's purchase, construction of the new building, and the hiring of more factory workers. Invoking an urban development tactic, the city called the infusion a "forgivable loan," which meant it would eventually be canceled, without repayment, if the Wunderlich Fibre Box Company stayed put long enough in St. Louis.[5] Thus does urban manufacturing persist, despite the closing of so many factories in American cities, including a complex of General Motors assembly plants in St. Louis that once employed five thousand people in the production of three different vehicles: a sports car, a van, and a pickup truck. They came off assembly lines in three adjacent, multistory buildings on the city's north side, not far from the Wunderlich factory. GM closed the complex in the 1990s, responding to increasing sales of imported cars.

But the big automaker wasn't done making vehicles near St. Louis. Soon after, it expanded an existing, more efficient assembly plant in Wentzville, Missouri. Vans and pickup trucks once assembled in north St. Louis henceforth were assembled in Wentzville, in a factory building whose machinery GM sold to the city government at a steep discount in exchange for steeply reduced property taxes and the right to continue to use the machinery in the manufacture of vehicles.[6] It is a factory with 3.7 million square feet of floor space, which is greater than the combined square footage of the three multistory buildings at the old north St. Louis factory complex. In Wentzville that square footage is on one vast floor and under one roof, simplifying assembly and reducing costs. The number of employees has risen to 2,200, of whom 35 percent were African Americans when I visited, according to Local 2250 of the United Auto Workers.[7] Most were from the Wentzville area, or from nearby communities. Very few commuted from north St. Louis, whose residents might have dominated the workforce if GM's expansion had taken place in their urban neighborhood—on now vacant land that goes begging for commerce of any sort.

Manufacturing once permeated St. Louis, particularly the north side, employing thousands of men and women who lived near the factories. The GM plant in particular drew employees from the large population of African Americans whose families had migrated from the South. As these autoworkers prospered, some moved up a notch to homes in the blue-collar suburbs just north of the city. When GM first opened its factory on the outskirts of Wentzville, in 1984, some hourly workers transferred to the spacious new facility from north St. Louis, commuting the sixty miles by car or moving nearer to the plant, causing Wentzville's rural population to balloon.[8]

But the mix is different from what it would have been if the company had put its new factory near the old one in north St. Louis, as GM itself initially proposed to do—if the city and state had been willing to provide sufficient support. That did not happen and GM moved out. Left behind were thousands of men and women who had never worked for GM, or in any well-paying factory job, but might have eventually landed work at the auto company if it had built a modern factory near their north-side homes, using a few acres of the plentifully available land. Instead, those who found work ended up mostly in service sector jobs that paid $10 to $15 an hour less than an auto factory would have paid an assembly line operator. And as time passes, and one generation succeeds another, the memory of what might have been is lost.

The decision to close the north St. Louis factory and deprive African Americans in the community of well-paying unionized factory jobs might well be viewed as a civil rights violation. Factories, like public schools, depend at least in part on taxpayer funding. They are semipublic institutions and for that reason should not be relocated (intentionally or not) out of the reach of African Americans, who are for the most part urban dwellers.

For at least a generation, however, manufacturers have migrated away from major cities, distancing themselves from African American neighborhoods that once helped to supply their urban factories with workers. The manufacturers left for good business reasons— a major one being more land on which to erect modern, more efficient, single-story factories. In both their old and new sites, however, they received subsidies. The subsidies, in turn, should obligate them to site their factories, if at all possible, in locations that maximize the opportunity for the employment of underrepresented groups, in particular African Americans—given their *overrepresentation* among the unemployed in that region. In GM's case, a number of African Americans already worked at the Wentzville plant, many of them having exercised a right in the United Auto Workers contract to transfer in from GM plants elsewhere in the country in the 1980s. I met the elected president of UAW Local 2250 in Wentzville, an African American man named Van Simpson, when I visited the plant in the fall of 2014. "We added a second shift in 1985," Simpson told me, "and in the hiring needed to man that shift we went to thirty percent black and seventy percent white from a nearly all-white workforce."[9] He himself had transferred in from the St. Louis factory.

Twenty-five years later, when that plant closed, African Americans working there also had the right to transfer to GM plants elsewhere in the country, and many did. But children whose parents or grandparents had had no connection to GM—children who continued to grow up in African American neighborhoods near the shuttered factory—were deprived of access to handsome hourly pay on a factory assembly line near their homes once they finished high school. "They got marooned, like fish gasping to breath in a pond nearly drained of water," is how Paul Wagman, a reporter for the *St. Louis Post-Dispatch* in the 1980s, put it years later.[10]

If there is consolation—bitter consolation—for the men and women left behind in urban ghettos, it consists in knowing that those who do replace them in auto factories that have been relocated away from big cities aren't so well off either. Starting in 2016, for example, an hourly worker hired at a GM plant anywhere in the country can be classified as a temporary employee earning a top salary, after four years, of only $19.28 an hour, or just $3.50 above the starting pay. By the fall of 2016, some one thousand workers at the Wentzville plant, or nearly one-quarter of the hourly workforce, were classified as "temps." Under the UAW contract incorporating this concessionary wage scale—a contract that went into effect in November 2015 without a strike—newly hired hourly workers could be kept in this temp classification for the first eight years of their employment. Only then do they rise to regular hourly employment. During those eight years, they can be required to work as many as six days a week, or as few as one, with any individual's schedule adjusted on fairly short notice to meet production requirements.[11]

Hard as this is, the old industrial neighborhoods are even worse off. They often deteriorate into boarded-up buildings or giant paved-over parking lots where factories once stood.[12] That is exactly what has happened in north St. Louis. Subsidized redevelopment has focused instead on an expanding complex of hospitals, clinics, offices, medical schools, laboratories, and related facilities located downtown and employing thousands of people who once might have earned more in factories nearer their homes. The numerous low-end jobs in this growing medical-research-office complex are in food and janitorial services, building maintenance, and as clerks, order-lies, ambulance drivers, nurses' aides, and the like. Their wages top out in most cases at less than $20 an hour. This notch down from factory assembly line work translates into a notch down in living standards—not for the doctors, scientists, and researchers in these new complexes, but for those employed to support them.

By the early twenty-first century, for example, more than eigh-teen thousand people worked in health care support jobs in St. Louis, according to the U.S. Census Bureau. Despite the downgrade in pay, the buildings in the new medical-research complexes in St. Louis and in other once-great industrial cities enhance and modernize de-teriorating downtowns. In St. Louis, these shiny multistory build-ings sweep westward from the Mississippi along a swath of streets half a dozen blocks wide. Driving along Forest Park Avenue in the spring of 2014, in the middle of this upgraded downtown, I passed twenty- to thirty-story buildings, beige and light-colored for the most part or sheathed in opaque glass. More were soon to be built on cleared land or were in the earliest stages of construction. The expanding concentration of medical and research facilities, inter-spersed with three or four corporate headquarters buildings, is closely allied to the city's biggest hospitals and to its two biggest universities, with their prestigious medical schools.[13] And there is another bonus: as not-for-profit organizations, the new medical research centers cannot legally distribute what are in effect their earnings, so they frequently invest the money in further expansion.

The result is what seems to me—on periodic visits to St. Louis—perpetual construction.

At the eastern end of all this activity, a soaring arch rises in a narrow park along the Mississippi River, gracefully welcoming people to the new St. Louis. Manufacturing once enriched this swath of the city. Wagman covered the wave of urban factory closings for the *Post-Dispatch* in the early 1980s that eventually changed the city. "I was writing their obituaries on a frequent basis," he recalled, "and over time people decided that we could never recover in manufacturing to where we had been, and the future lay in biotechnology." But a biotechnology future comes with an ironic caveat: the hope is that all the research will produce a breakthrough drug, like penicillin in the 1940s, or some other popular medical product, which will then be manufactured in St. Louis, generating jobs and paychecks on a grand scale, just as manufacturing once did. The prototype is Silicon Valley and, as in Silicon Valley, there is much talk of incubators and start-ups.

Beyond the horizon of biotechnology—should that vision not be realized—real estate development is waiting in the wings to maximize the economic potential of formerly industrialized districts of the city. This means putting high-end apartments and condominiums on the many acres where factories often stood, as well as the homes of men and women who worked in the factories. An accountant could argue, accurately, that the money earned on a dollar invested in a square foot of an apartment building, a condominium, an office tower, a hospital, or a research facility is greater than the return on a dollar invested in a square foot of factory. That greater return (or the expectation of it) helps to explain the blossoming of these alternatives. In New York, for example, a stretch of thirty square blocks that includes disused railroad tracks along the Hudson River in midtown Manhattan has gradually shifted from commercial and factory use to residential apartments. In 2014, Tutor Perini, a giant construction company headquartered in Las Vegas, was building or planning to build apartments and condominiums in the area for five thousand residents who will pay, on average, $6,000 per square foot. Peter Sukalo, a senior vice president of Tutor Perini, told me the $6,000-per-square-foot payoff is more than five times greater than the cost of purchasing the land and developing it into a residential complex.[14] The potential profit, in other words, is four dollars or more for every dollar invested.

Such lucrative profits skew urban redevelopment away from manufacturing, a larger and steadier source of blue-collar employment over the long run than the construction jobs that disappear when a project is completed. Pursuing the same rich return in St. Louis, the real estate developer Paul McKee gradually purchased land in north St. Louis for $35,000 an acre on average, accumulating 1,500 acres over a decade.[15] His stated plan was to invest $390 million—all of it borrowed—to build apartments and condominiums, and then take in more than $8 billion, or sixteen times his investment, as he sold off the properties.[16]

By McKee's estimate, forty thousand people once lived on the land that he and his wife, Midge, had gradually acquired. Their homes are mostly gone, and so are the stores they frequented, but not the marked-off plots where many of those homes and stores once stood, or the streets that divided the land into plots and, in McKee's plan, would serve the residents of his real estate development—before he gave up on the project. Also gone are the GM factories that stood next to one another along the northern edge of this neighborhood, employing a number of those former residents. Others had worked at a big Rexall factory near the GM complex—also closed— or at smaller factories in the neighborhood, some of them dedicated to making parts for the vehicles assembled in the GM factories. Most of these shops went out of business or were moved elsewhere when GM departed.

Paul and Midge McKee, coming in after this exodus, gambled that they could turn once-busy factory neighborhoods into neighborhoods of office workers who would commute by car to jobs in St. Louis or Illinois from his strategically located residential community, which he got started developing with relatively little upfront cost to himself. Recently built sections of Interstate 70 skirted his land and a new bridge carried the highway's traffic over the Mississippi into Illinois. "It's the third-longest bridge in the world," McKee said, by way of explaining to me that the breadwinners in the homes he would build could commute easily to jobs in Illinois.[17]

Very few of the homes that McKee envisioned were ever built on the 360 building-size parcels that he accumulated. He went broke, and three years later, in 2016, the scrubland was still mostly scrubland. What saved McKee, or promised to do so, was the National Geospatial-Intelligence Agency, which decided to relocate from downtown St. Louis to a larger site within the city—one that included the parcels he owned. Payment came, or was scheduled to come, from a $20 million loan to the agency from the City of St. Louis, approved by its aldermen in 2015.[18]

The factories that continue to function within St. Louis remain in place because the owners prefer to stay put, as Robert Wunderlich has chosen to do, although more than a few of those who purchase his corrugated fiberboard containers have moved their factories to other, less urban locations. Serving them means hauling the folded, flattened containers on tractor-trailers to the new sites, which is feasible if the distance is no more than 150 miles. Beyond that, the cost of trucking becomes too great. "If I have a good customer and he moves too far away, I have to give him up to a competitor or move myself," Wunderlich said.[19] The Wunderlichs have resisted the idea of opening a second or third factory closer to the new locations of their migrating customers, a tactic that could mean closing or shrinking the St. Louis operation, with its sixty employees, and repaying the forgivable loan.

So the Wunderlichs have stayed put. For thousands of other urban manufacturers, however, staying put ceased to be a viable option in the 1970s. Seeking to expand, they acquired additional acreage away from cities for the more efficient single-story factories that were becoming the norm. And transportation infrastructure helped them. Until the 1950s, rivers and railroads carried most factory-made merchandise, and these routes connected cities, making the latter very good places to put factories, particularly in the Midwest. With the construction of the interstate highway system, that restriction gradually disappeared. Factories went up along the wide new highways, which in many cases were near cities but not in them, and tractor-trailer trucks handled more and more of the transportation. When he was a newcomer to the family business more than thirty years ago, Robert Wunderlich noticed the shift and suggested to his father that they move to new and larger quarters in a more rural setting. "I said, 'Dad, we should get out of here,'" the son recalled. He did not want to go far from St. Louis, but far enough to acquire the necessary land for an ample single-story building, with acreage left over for future expansion. The lure of lower-wage nonunion labor in smaller cities and towns also influenced him.[20] Yet his father, who had come of age when St. Louis was a huge manufacturing center, nixed the idea, and Wunderlich hewed to its urban roots.

The range of products made in St. Louis a century or so ago is hard to imagine today. The city's numerous factories produced organs, pianos, paper, beer, furniture, mattresses, window frames, watches, toys, iron and steel, textiles, hats, boots and shoes, millinery, streetcars, railroad freight cars, carpets, agricultural machinery, cars, stoves, furnaces, display cases, photographic plates, door hinges, pharmaceuticals, and deep-red bricks—a characteristic building material in St. Louis until the nearby clay deposits ran low in the late twentieth century.[21]

Most of these factories were family owned for many years, usually started by an enterprising immigrant or a young American drawn to the obvious industrial potential of St. Louis, with its sophisticated transportation network. Some of the companies were the nation's largest producers of a particular product for a while. No other city, for example, manufactured more streetcars and railroad freight cars in the early twentieth century—and St. Louis preceded Detroit as a center of auto production.[22]

Even today, two iconic manufacturing operations are still located, amazingly, in downtown St. Louis. In a complex of seven interconnected multistory buildings occupying nearly a square city block and constructed over nearly fifty years as the company grew, all of the Tums antacid tablets sold in the western hemisphere are made.[23] "In the 1990s, we considered moving to a greenfield site outside the city," said Stephen Bishop, the now retired site director for the St. Louis operation, "and we concluded that there would be no advantage gained from investing the huge amount that would be required. There would be no product improvement."[24]

A few blocks away, Anheuser-Busch operates an automated brewery that produces thousands of bottles and cans of beer every hour, each one bobbing along the line as if it were a miniature person walking toward an exit at a steady pace.[25] Not many assembly lines in the country are more efficient than the Anheuser-Busch operation, located on the company's original site, where the brewery was founded in 1852.[26] But in the same neighborhood, buildings that once housed first-rate factories go begging for tenants, raising the question: Given the success of Anheuser-Busch and Tums, not to mention small operations such as Wunderlich, should the subsidies devoted to the expansion of the medical and scientific complex go instead to modern factories—or should they go to modern factories at least as often as to medical and scientific facilities? In the case of Anheuser-Busch, should it have gone its current route, putting additional breweries elsewhere in the country, or should it have greatly expanded its brewery in St. Louis and shipped beer in bulk to satellite packagers around the country?[27] Subsidies could have made that happen.

Put more insistently: Is manufacturing a better means—even the best means—of enriching cities and lifting the wages of urban workers? I would argue that it is, on two grounds: manufacturing benefits cities, which tax away a share of the sector's value added; and it benefits workers, particularly unionized workers, who use their leverage to collect a sizeable share of the value added, through collective bargaining.[28] Over the decades, in fact, urban factory workers have led the nation in achieving higher wages and other benefits for blue-collar workers. The union movement, after all, originated in cities, and urban factory workers still largely sustain it.

The Wunderlichs, sticking with St. Louis, almost ran out of heirs to take over in the current generation. The family patriarch, Robert A. Wunderlich, continued to run the company into his late seventies, mainly because he was in good health and liked doing so, but also because his son, Robert Jr., a U.S. Marine Corps pilot, was reluctant to leave the service. As Robert Sr. told the story, his son finally shifted to the reserves, under pressure from his father, so that he could join the business, gain experience, and extend family ownership to a sixth generation. "He could not have made the kind of salary in the military that he makes here," Robert Sr. explained to me, "and if he had not come into the company, there might not be a sixth generation."[29]

When I met Robert Jr. in September of 2016, at the Wunderlich operation in north St. Louis, I realized, twenty minutes into the conversation, that the sixth generation had already taken over. I had expected his father to do the talking and the son to listen quietly, a reluctant captive of the family business. But Robert Jr. dominated the conversation almost immediately and it was soon clear from the way others in the company dealt with this tall and genial man that he was already running things. At age fifty, he still piloted Boeing KC-135 Stratotankers a couple of times a month—tanker planes that refuel jet fighters in midair—but that could be a problem. "Last year, when I was deployed to Qatar," the son told me, "I was able to send e-mails to customers saying 'Greetings from Qatar.' But if a customer received a shipment of faulty boxes and needed help right away, I needed to be in St. Louis. I couldn't be in Qatar."

With Robert Jr. finally in place in 2016, his father anticipated the continued support of the city for the factory in north St. Louis. First and foremost, the family sought land nearby on which to build a warehouse, and save the rent paid for one across the Mississippi River, in Illinois. The necessary vacant land is available a block or two from the factory—land that had once been part of a busy commercial neighborhood. Its private owners asked too high a price, the Wunderlichs said, and they couldn't afford it unless the city government stepped in and, in effect, subsidized the purchase.

In exchange for past and present support, the city has pressed the Wunderlichs to hire St. Louis residents, mostly unemployed African Americans, including some who live near the factory. It has even sent candidates for interviews. "The city has an agency that we are required to contact whenever we have an opening," Robert Sr. explained, referring to the St. Louis Agency on Training and Employment. "We have hired one or two of these people, but mostly they are unqualified." Rather than train them, Wunderlich turned elsewhere, recruiting people from blue-collar suburbs just north of the city or from Illinois, directly across the river. On one visit, Robert Sr. showed me several cars with Illinois plates in the factory's parking lot, which is surrounded by a high chain-link fence—for protection from vandalism, as he put it. The recruits included African Americans who have managed to move to better residential areas just beyond city limits. "These people are middle-class blue collar," Robert Sr. said. In contrast, people in the neighborhood, around the factory itself, are often destitute and alone, living in halfway houses rather than in homes and apartments. Yet of course they too need good jobs, as do those in similar neighborhoods in other cities. Should manufacturers who receive government subsidies to operate urban factories be required, in exchange for those subsidies, to hire men and women from neighborhoods near the factories, training them as necessary to bring their skills up to par, even if that means resettling people in decent housing? Through court rulings and legislation, we have outlawed racial discrimination in public places. But we have not defined factories as public places, or at least as semipublic places, although that is what they are, given the various subsidies that provide vital support.

In exchange for these subsidies, the courts should require that manufacturers locate more factories in north St. Louis and in similar urban neighborhoods. And the city should welcome their return. After all, it was mass-production factories with their tens of thousands of assembly line jobs that converted St. Louis into a massive, complex industrial city generating wages and wealth far beyond what the current generation of hospitals, research centers, office buildings, and high-tech companies is likely to achieve. The Big Three automakers—GM, Ford, and Chrysler—all assembled cars in St. Louis; none do so now. The numerous hat and shoe factories are gone, although the names of some still appear in faded paint high on the walls of buildings they once occupied. The formerly numerous steel mills have disappeared from St. Louis as well.

Dr. Donald Suggs, an African American dentist and community leader, knew manufacturing's heyday in the Midwest firsthand. His father had come north to an assembly line job at a steel mill near Chicago, and his children, leveraging their father's steady income, went further. Dr. Suggs became an oral surgeon. When I first met him, in 2014, he had retired from that profession but had continued as publisher of the weekly *St. Louis American* newspaper, circulated mainly to black readers. From that perch, he described the draining away of factory jobs in cities such as St. Louis as a reversal of the opportunities that had brought his father and so many others north in the first place. "McDonnell-Douglas had forty thousand factory workers in St. Louis and many were African Americans," he said. "You lost those jobs and you also lost steel, and that has had implications for black people." As we talked in a conference room at his newspaper, on a return visit two years later, the "implications" became clear. His nearly illiterate father's factory job, thanks to a union contract, generated enough income and benefits for Dr. Suggs to finish high school and go on to college, then dental school. His children are similarly educated and successful, all thanks to that initial footing in factory work. "If my father had not had that job, at Inland Steel, working sixteen-hour days, five days a week during World War II, there would have been no basis for holding the family together." Nor would there have been patients for his dentistry. "My own practice as an oral surgeon was successful based on servicing factory workers and their families," he explained. "Now, with so many factories gone, a practice like mine can't exist anymore." Given their importance, I asked why the cutback in relatively well-paying factory jobs in recent years had not sparked protests reminiscent of the civil rights movement in the 1960s. His answer was disheartening: "The civil rights movement opened the door slightly for a certain group of people who moved up and out, and this has taken away a lot of the energy and the activism that is needed to help the African American underclass."[30]

My first visit to the Wunderlich factory took place on an overcast August day, contributing to the impression of a deteriorating industrial neighborhood.[31] While some factories still operated at full tilt, many of the buildings that other manufacturers once occupied were empty or underutilized—or they have been converted into warehouses or torn down and the sites leveled until a better use for the land comes along. Urban redevelopment, meanwhile, diverts attention from the unsightliness of this wasted land in many American cities. It is doing so in spectacular fashion in St. Louis, particularly along Forest Park Avenue, stretching west from the silvery arch on the Mississippi River. But the energy and bustle that factory production and abundant transportation helped to generate is gone, and so is the excitement that I once felt on excursions downtown.

Granted, I was young and impressionable on those early excursions in the mid-twentieth century during visits to my grandparents, who lived in a Victorian house near a trolley line that took commuters, including my grandfather, to the center of the city in thirty minutes. He and my grandmother had settled in St. Louis in 1905 as newlyweds and had raised three children; my mother was the eldest. She had gone east to college, married a New Yorker, and raised four children in a New York suburb. But her family and friends in St. Louis, and the city itself, lured her home for periodic visits, often with one or more of her children in tow.

Later, as teenagers, we made the overnight train trip on our own, traveling on the crack (for those days) Spirit of St. Louis, which took us rapidly west through farmland and industrial cities in Pennsylvania, Ohio, Indiana, and Illinois before slowing to a crawl on the Illinois side of the Mississippi River, next to other trains that were also inching forward in a vast yard whose numerous tracks converged on Eads Bridge, the main river crossing for passenger trains. For an hour or so we barely moved, until it was our turn to cross. Once across—and free of the bottleneck—we moved hastily along in an underground tunnel, surfacing in time to pull up to one of the numerous roofed-over platforms extending out from Union Station, a massive limestone building that served a hundred thousand passengers a day in the mid-twentieth century.

The station itself is still intact, as is the neo-Romanesque clock tower that rises above it—quaint reminders of an active industrial past. In the early years of the twenty-first century the few Amtrak passenger trains coming through St. Louis each day loaded and unloaded their passengers two blocks away, in a nondescript building that doubled as a bus terminal. Union Station itself had become a giant indoor mall, serving only one commuter line from near-in suburbs and using for this purpose just a fraction of the huge station. The paved-over tracks had become a parking lot, and between the parking lot and the building there was a square pool, perhaps two hundred feet on each side and just deep enough for oversize goldfish and shallow-draft, two-seater paddle boats that could be rented for ten-minute spins. Several park benches and potted trees around the pool tried to suggest an outdoor setting rather than a roofed-over one. Most of the wall space in the cavernous building was lined with small stores when I visited in 2014—some not much larger than stalls, selling handbags, St. Louis Cardinals clothing and memorabilia, decorative T-shirts and sweatshirts, souvenirs, colorful handbags, junk food, and more. Yet another pool, circular and fountain-like, served as a wishing well, for tossing coins into. An artist offered to sketch my face in charcoal. And a cement-colored hotel recently built next to the station marketed its rooms mainly to tourists who had traveled to St. Louis by car or airliner, not by train. What remained from the industrial past at Union Station was the giant opaque roof extending outward from the station, sheltering the parking lot covering the tracks that had brought me to St. Louis as a boy.

Two years later, the parking lot was gone. So were the shops and the stalls, as well as the pools, the goldfish, and the paddleboats. The sign over the main entrance to the station now said Union Station Hotel rather than just Union Station. A carpeted staircase with ornate, dark wooden banisters, rising from the main entrance, opened onto the Grand Hall, a vast reception room with a long, cream-colored bar along one wall where ticket windows or gates to waiting trains once had been. Numerous couches and coffee tables filled the enormous hall, carefully arranged so that people could gather in small groups for drinks and snacks. Meeting rooms had been added in other areas of the huge building as Union Station completed the transition to convention center hotel. Outdoors, the giant opaque roof sheltered six or seven railroad passenger cars built in the 1950s and 1960s, before air travel finally replaced the long-distance trains that linked the nation's cities. The cars were now tourist attractions, particularly the dining car.

Back in the mid-twentieth century, freight trains, like passenger trains, also moved underground after crossing the Mississippi, but they headed to Cupples Station, a freight terminal surrounded by nearly a dozen multistoried structures solidly built of stone or brick.[32] These buildings once housed factories and warehouses. The first auto manufacturers got started in this neighborhood, before production shifted en masse to Detroit and left these buildings underutilized except for a few corporate headquarters, the most visible being Ralston Purina, whose executives, as of 2016, still ran the multinational corporation from a fifteen-story building, sheathed in white, that stood out on a sunny day like a brightly shining skyscraper in a neighborhood of shorter, dull-colored structures. In 1894, William H. Danforth, then only twenty-four years old, founded Ralston-Purina in St. Louis as an animal-feed manufacturer—a natural for a river port city in the grain belt. By the end of the twentieth century, however, the actual manufacture of animal feed and pet food had moved elsewhere. "The company wanted to build large new factories on more land than the city had available," said Ruth Keenoy, a preservation specialist at the Landmarks Association of St. Louis, "but they still wanted to keep their headquarters in the city."[33] In the process, hundreds of blue-collar jobs were eliminated, while many of the remaining white-collar workers commuted from the suburbs. The result has been fewer people on downtown streets, which was not the goal of urban redevelopment in St. Louis or in other once-great industrial cities. Redevelopment was supposed to keep people downtown after work, or draw them from the suburbs to attend sports events in a new stadium and gather for musical performances at a new symphony hall, each built partly with public subsidies. In the absence of manufacturing, the thinking went, cities should make downtown a place for sports events, concerts, dining, socializing, and shopping.

That has not happened. Redevelopment has failed to bring back the crowded streets and the vibrant commerce of the industrial city that I knew on those visits to my grandparents as a boy and later as a student at the University of Michigan in the 1950s, when I would sometimes travel in the Midwest during school breaks and, when I did, I invariably found myself jostled in the crowded downtowns of Cincinnati, Cleveland, Indianapolis, or St. Louis. Factories brought those downtowns to life, and factory workers lived near them. When I returned to those cities in the 1990s, as a reporter on assignments for the *New York Times*, the vibrancy was gone except during the morning and evening commutes. By all accounts, the exodus started with the departure of upper-middle-class families for the suburbs. Manufacturers followed suit in the 1970s and 1980s, leaving behind thousands of people who had worked in urban factories, living near them. Most of these workers left as well, following their employers and compounding the migration. With relatively few exceptions, the migrants were white families. De facto segregation, enforced by real estate agents, prevented African American families from moving as easily. Many stayed put in increasingly impoverished neighborhoods. Without the factories and the suppliers that served them, fewer jobs at decent pay remained for the residents of these ghettos.

As for the manufacturers, their exodus took place in stages. Seeking initially to expand or modernize their operations, or both, they migrated to towns that offered enough land to meet their needs, as well as men and women who expected lower wages than their urban counterparts. That was Fred Epstein's explanation for why his father, Milton Epstein, decided in the late 1950s to move the business that Milton and a brother had started in downtown St. Louis in 1929, first as distributors of commercial heating units and then as manufacturers of electrical devices that heat air pumped through building ducts. Thirty years later, they needed more space for their expanding operation, formally called the Industrial Engineering and Equipment Company (INDEECO for short). Unable to acquire the additional land near their existing factory, the Epsteins moved production in 1959 to the still rural town of Brentwood, about fifteen miles away, building a factory on a large plot that the town donated to the company, happy to have the jobs and the commercial activity that INDEECO generated.

"The city of St. Louis wasn't interested in helping us," Epstein said of that first move. In 1963, however, the Teamsters organized most of INDEECO's 225 workers in Brentwood and, partly in response, Epstein moved most of his operation even farther out, to factories in the smaller Missouri towns of Boonville and Cuba. The Brentwood factory building remained in the family's hands, some of it leased to other companies. "The primary reason for this second migration was to lower our labor costs, and another reason was to avoid the hassle of having to deal with labor unions," he explained. "The Teamsters tried to organize our Boonville staff and they failed."[34]

A quest for less militant and less expensive workers led many manufacturers to migrate from urban centers like St. Louis to smaller communities that also offered plenty of land to build modern, single-story factories. "We needed more land to grow," Epstein said, mentioning but not dwelling on the subsidies embedded in the offers communities made as they competed to convince companies such as INDEECO to move to one town rather than another. The gift of free land from the municipal government in Brentwood, and later from the City of Boonville in central Missouri, certainly constituted public subsidies and reduced the overall cost of the factories that Epstein agreed to build.[35] In that long process of relocating serially from St. Louis to Brentwood to Boonville and Cuba, he shrank by one-third the cost of wages and benefits from the level they would have reached if INDEECO had stayed in St. Louis.[36] The subsidies that came with each move literally bought lower wages. That process of using subsidies to cut wages and weaken unions repeats itself constantly in the United States as hundreds of economic development organizations, each one connected to a municipal government, hold out the likelihood of lowered wages as a reason for a company to locate a factory, a headquarters, an office building, or some other labor-intensive operation in a particular community. Yet this constant, subsidized migration has rarely if ever been challenged in the courts on the ground that it is anti-union or anti-labor, or even in violation of the Wagner Act, although that is what it may be.[37]

Eventually Epstein offered his four children a successful and profitable family business to own and run for yet another generation. They declined, and their father was not all that disappointed—in part because Fred Epstein himself was ambivalent about his own career. He had graduated from the Massachusetts Institute of Technology with a degree in physics but never pursued a career in that field, instead joining the family business right out of MIT in the early 1950s, representing the third generation of Epsteins in the company. "I wanted a good income and the flexibility that comes with owning my own business so I could get involved civically," he explained. And he did get involved, joining the American Civil Liberties Union and rising through its ranks, serving first on its national board and then on its executive board. It was a parallel career that seemed to contribute at least as much to his self-esteem as owning and running INDEECO.

Once Epstein's children had made clear to their father that they would not follow in his footsteps, the father, then in his early seventies, put INDEECO up for sale. And a private equity firm stepped in, purchasing yet another American factory and combining its operation with a similar factory already in the firm's portfolio—eliminating duplication, of course, but diluting yet again the role that factories play in the employment of high school–educated men and women. In this case, the buyer was ASPEQ Heating Group, which billed itself as specializing in the purchase of small manufacturing companies within 250 miles of St. Louis.[38] Private equity firms have become major owners of American manufacturers over the past thirty years, and they have contributed to the departure of those companies from U.S. cities—and from the nation as well, in some cases.

On the day I met Epstein, in August 2013, five years after he had sold INDEECO, he drove me out to the old Brentwood plant, where ASPEQ had set up its offices, and introduced me to John Eulich, who was simultaneously the chairman of ASPEQ and also of INDEECO, the private equity firm's first acquisition. Eulich, an engineer in his mid-forties with a Harvard MBA, took over the interview while Epstein listened, injecting his views from time to time and occasionally leaving the small conference room while Eulich and I talked.

When he became interested in INDEECO, Eulich said, it had already shifted most of its production from Brentwood to non-union plants in rural Missouri, a cost-cutting tactic that had appealed to him, contributing to his decision to acquire the company. I wondered, for the sake of argument, what might prompt him to reverse course and reopen a factory in St. Louis. What if—by some miracle—wages declined to rural Missouri levels and the city came through with handsome subsidies? "No," he replied, "I would not move back. The biggest cost is attracting and training a workforce, and then once I've got three hundred people in place in St. Louis, someone's going to say, 'Let's organize a union.'"

Twenty years ago, William Julius Wilson, the prominent African American scholar at Harvard, recognized the tragedy that was developing as manufacturers closed their urban factories and migrated away from cities. In his classic book *When Work Disappears: The World of the New Urban Poor*, he wrote, "The manufacturing [job] losses in some northern cities have been staggering. In the twenty-year period from 1967 to 1987, Philadelphia lost 64 percent of its manufacturing jobs; Chicago lost 60 percent; New York City, 58 percent; Detroit, 51 percent."[39] And African American workers and their families were hit the hardest.[40] Wilson could have added St. Louis, which lost at least 50 percent of its manufacturing jobs in the same period. If he were updating his book, he would report that what he found in the late 1990s is still the case in the twenty-first century in many American cities.

Why not explicitly and publicly link the exodus of manufacturers from our cities to the high unemployment rates among African Americans living in urban neighborhoods—and emphasize the connection until it is common knowledge? Why not also publicly question why this should be allowed to happen, given that manufacturers are almost always subsidized, and therefore have—or should have—an obligation to explain their actions to the public, which supplies their subsidies through taxes?

Instead, in a grotesque distortion of supply-side economics, we blame working-age people themselves for the departure of manufacturers from urban neighborhoods. The blame falls particularly on African Americans: if only they would get themselves educated, this line of reasoning goes, jobs would materialize. That is simply not true. Skill in manufacturing exists separately from formal education, as we saw in chapter 2, and manufacturers migrating from urban centers have left behind black men and women who could have skillfully staffed their factories but can't easily relocate out of their home city.

One result has been a soaring unemployment rate among urban blacks. Another has been the persistence of a racist rhetoric claiming that black people on welfare lose the incentive to work, or were shiftless to begin with. The political scientist Charles Murray became the most prominent advocate of this view in his widely circulated book *Losing Ground*, published in 1984.[41] It shows up to this day in the political rhetoric of some politicians, mainly Republicans such as the speaker of the House, Representative Paul Ryan of Wisconsin, who has attributed persistent poverty to "a culture, in our inner cities in particular, of men not working and just generations of men not even thinking of working."[42]

The decline of manufacturing had a multiplier effect, bringing with it the collapse of numerous urban enterprises linked to manufacturing, which in turn eliminated additional jobs and skills. These included legions of wholesalers and retailers who distributed and sold manufactured products, moving them in steps from factories to consumers. My grandfather, Lee Cronbach, owned such an enterprise, a tobacco store on Olive Street near the Mississippi River, a few blocks from Union Station. Visiting the store as a boy, I would find him behind the counter, in a gray or navy-blue suit and—always—a white shirt and tie, waiting on a customer himself if the regular sales clerks were busy. His income, however, came mainly from a larger and less visible business, and over the years I came to think of the store as his office for that larger business and the display counters as his desk in that office.[43]

Like many independent retailers in those days, my grandfather had a stake in some of the products he sold, in his case proprietary brands of cigar and pipe tobacco, some manufactured in this country, at factories in Tampa and in the Midwest, and others made over-seas.[44] He distributed the cigars and the pipe tobacco from a warehouse he leased in St. Louis, and he kept a considerable sup-ply in a walk-in humidor at the Olive Street store. Traveling sales-men, earning commissions, roamed the Midwest on his behalf, signing up customers (often small-town retailers) for his proprietary products: Emanelo cigars and Hayward Mixture pipe tobacco. My grandfather rarely advertised, and never in a big way, although his brands had some national recognition. Bing Crosby, the pipe-smoking actor and crooner, favored Hayward Mixture, which he received by mail from the warehouse.

The surgeon general's report in 1964, linking smoking and can-cer, would have eventually killed my grandfather's business, al-though the report concentrated on evidence connecting cigarettes to the disease rather than cigars and pipe tobacco. But even before the surgeon general, big national corporations had begun to pur-chase urban companies such as Moss & Lowenhaupt and absorb their function as regional distributors of proprietary tobacco prod-ucts. In my grandfather's case, the Universal Cigar Company pur-chased Moss & Lowenhaupt, reducing his business to a retail operation, so that it was no longer a distributor of factory-made to-bacco products.

The setbacks inflicted on urban populations, as manufacturers migrated from major American cities and big corporations absorbed the distribution operations of companies like my grandfather's, did not have to happen. The same government money that helped to finance the modern skyscrapers that now shape the skylines of so many of our downtowns could have been used to keep manufacturers and distributors rooted in the cities by helping them pay for their operations—with the proviso that these subsidized companies employ mostly urban residents.

That was the unspoken tragedy in Ferguson, the St. Louis suburb where rioting and protests erupted in the summer of 2014 after a white police officer shot and killed Michael Brown, a black teenager who had recently graduated from Normandy High School. While Brown had been headed for Vatterott College, a local technical school that offered degrees in the repair and maintenance of heating units, air conditioners, and other machinery, most of his Normandy classmates did not continue their education. In the past, that had not been a problem. They had often rolled out of Normandy High into hourly assembly line jobs at Emerson Electric. But Emerson had closed factories in St. Louis, the city of its birth, and had put them elsewhere in the country. For a while in the late twentieth century, in fact, Emerson factories in the Ferguson area were that community's main employer, along with the now-gone Ford and GM plants in nearby north St. Louis. By the twenty-first century, however, only Emerson's corporate headquarters remained in Ferguson, on a rolling green campus on the outskirts of the city.[45]

The slow hollowing out of America's formerly industrial cities has seemed like an inexorable, natural process. The Scullin Steel works in the northwestern outskirts of St. Louis was once a huge employer of African Americans whose families had migrated north to St. Louis. It is closed now, and gone—the land given over to a big shopping center and a gasoline station. Only the headquarters building remains. "Scullin Steel" is still carved into the granite over the front entrance. The building itself, however, was home to a copier company when I visited, in 2014 and again in 2016, one that sold, leased, and repaired copy machines.[46] The nearby National Lead Company is also closed, as is the St. Louis Arms and Ammunition factory, which occupied a large track just north of Scullin, not far from a Monsanto plant. Monsanto, the giant agrochemical and agricultural biotechnology company, is still, like Brown Shoe, headquartered in St. Louis, where it was founded in 1901, and still does much of its research not far away. But its production facilities, like Brown's, are located elsewhere.[47] Most of the Monsanto factories were relocated in the 1970s and 1980s, but some left as far back as the 1950s—early casualties in St. Louis's long decline as an industrial city and as a source of racially integrated blue-collar factory employment.

Yet, bucking the migration, at least in St. Louis, and demonstrating day-in and day-out the viability of urban manufacturing, the Anheuser-Busch brewery and the Tums complex a few streets away are vivid reminders of the city's prosperous industrial age. Huge sums have been sunk into the Tums operation and the Anheuser brewery over the decades; shutting them down would mean having to spend huge sums again on replacement factories elsewhere. If that is the case for Anheuser-Busch and Tums, why let any manufacturer leave town without a thorough vetting of the company's reasons weighed against the needs of the city being left behind?

Acknowledging the power of subsidies must be the starting point. In exchange for subsidies, should the nation's manufacturers, particularly the big ones, such as Anheuser-Busch, Tums, and GM, be required to locate some of their factories in major cities such as St. Louis? Should they be required to hire locally (which would offer significant employment opportunities to urban African American communities)? Finally, in exchange for subsidies, should they be required to recognize labor unions as legitimate bargaining agents for hourly factory workers?

That's a lot of *shoulds*. Some wouldn't survive court challenges, but they would bend public awareness toward a recognition of manufacturing as a subsidized activity with social obligations. And that recognition—the intertwining of subsidies, civil rights, and urban well-being—would be a healthier dynamic than the current one, in which manufacturers get state and local governments to bid against each other for their presence. Whatever the scenario, the alternative for a city that loses its factories is often bleak. Public money may be spent on the beautifying of former industrial neighborhoods, in the form of sleek office towers, new stadiums and cultural centers, and, in the case of St. Louis, the dramatic arch in a picturesque riverside park. What cannot be replaced is the dynamism, as well as the employment, the energy, and the exhilaration that manufacturing generates and that I knew on visits to St. Louis as a teenager and a young man.

4

Subsidies

The National Association of Manufacturers, representing most of the nation's factory owners, meets every year in Washington in late spring. It is a curious two-day gathering. The NAM calls it a "manufacturing summit," and certainly the nearly five hundred chief executives and corporate chairmen who attended the 2014 summit were representative of the nation's factory owners at the highest level. But they shrank from calling attention to themselves. No grand luncheon or black-tie dinner-dance or visit to the Oval Office celebrated their presence, although on the first morning they gathered in a giant ballroom at the Renaissance Hotel for a pep talk from Vice President Joe Biden, who declared: "Where is it written that America will not lead the world in manufacturing in the 21st Century?"[1] To hear Biden tell it, manufacturing in America is a perennial success and it owes that success to hard work, ingenuity, resourcefulness; good highways, air freight, and railroads; abundant energy, skilled workers, robust exports, the world's best research universities, and a knack for innovation which, Biden told his audience, "is stamped into your DNA." As a manufacturing nation "we're incredibly well positioned," he concluded in a nine-page speech that failed to single out subsidies, or even mention them. The manufacturers heard him out, applauded of course, and then they were off—to visit with those who have the power to disburse subsidies. Chartered buses parked outside the hotel shuttled them—like troops aboard landing craft—the seventeen blocks to the Capitol, where they disembarked, entered the building, and met in small groups with members of Congress, seeking their help for one project or another, or federal support for manufacturing in general.[2] When they were done, the buses shuttled the manufacturing chieftains back to the hotel, making several roundtrips each day.

The NAM is skilled at public relations. It employs half a dozen professionals to publicize manufacturing in the United States, and it posts on its website press releases that beat the drums for the positions that manufacturers favor. But it shies away from spotlighting subsidies in a nation whose political leaders, like Biden, encourage the public to focus on self-sufficiency and innovative genius. Since the NAM's spring meeting is mainly about leavening self-sufficiency with the pursuit of subsidies, journalists don't get a lot of encouragement to cover the event. The handful who did in 2014 were given cordoned-off seats for the vice president's speech, with its Horatio Alger message, but were kept off the shuttle buses and away from the hat-in-hand visits with members of Congress.

There are very few manufacturers in the United States who operate without a public subsidy of some sort, and they often hire lobbyists to help secure them. Added together, subsidies pay for 20 percent of what the nation's factories produce, or $780 billion of the $4 trillion in output.[3] The manufacturers themselves acknowledge the help they get from government, if you ask them. But only after numerous interviews over more than twenty years as a reporter for the *New York Times* did I gradually come to realize that government subsidies, in cash or in kind, support not just manufacturing in general, but almost every manufacturer individually. The manufacturers often speak of the market-driven, competitive aspects of their activities while playing down, or taking for granted, the public support they receive, and often need, to stay profitably afloat. If innovation is stamped into the DNA of the nation's manufacturers, so are subsidies—broadly defined to include all the public money paid out to support factory production (highways, for example) or to purchase what factories produce (weapons for the armed forces, for example, or police cars for cities).

Brazen though that claim may sound, we may finally have distanced ourselves sufficiently from the ideological struggles of the twentieth century to acknowledge government's essential participation in manufacturing, without a chorus insisting that subsidies taint and degrade the American market system. They don't. They supplement it, and have done so in manufacturing going all the way back to 1791, when Alexander Hamilton published his *Report on the Subject of Manufactures,* in which he argued that the people of the newly formed United States required "the aid of their own government" to offset the "bounties" that governments in other countries gave their manufacturers.[4] That support has continued to this day for a more essential reason. Manufacturing isn't just a market activity; given its complexity, government must help, and it does so through subsidies that sustain this vital activity. That happens not only in the United States but in any nation with a substantial manufacturing industry.[5]

Biden did not say that in his speech to the manufacturing executives in the spring of 2014. Nor did he do so in subsequent speeches. Perhaps for him—for any vice president of the United States in the early twenty-first century—the perception of subsidies cannot be disentangled from failed ideology, or from the persistent belief, among a significant number of Americans, that government gets in the way. After all, millions of people vote for candidates who advocate lower taxes, less public spending, and a minimally regulated, hands-off market system in which corporations generate wealth and profits on their own. In this theoretical world, ingenuity, resourcefulness, and innovative genius yield success, and Biden praised his audience of executives for having these qualities. His audience applauded the fiction, but knew better. After all, they had traveled to Washington to lobby for subsidies, in particular for reauthorization of the Export–Import Bank, which was due to expire soon. Without the bank's low-cost financing, the manufacturers would find themselves with fewer overseas customers who could afford to purchase what the manufacturers sought to export.[6]

This vital government role isn't convenient for any administration to acknowledge. As the old ideologies continue to wear away, however, a vice president of the United States, making a similar speech at the NAM's spring conference in, say, 2024, might very well argue in favor of public subsidies to keep manufacturing not only afloat but also on the cutting edge and prosperous. One can even imagine that in the presidential election campaign that year, each candidate will insist that his or her party administers subsidies more effectively and more generously than the other—targeting them, for example, toward manufacturers who maintain factories in ghetto neighborhoods, or who put new ones in such neighborhoods, employing African Americans living nearby, in effect addressing the civil rights issue described in chapter 3.

In our own times, however, the nation's presidents, going back to the 1970s, have focused very little public attention on the key role of government in sustaining factory output, not only in cities but in the nation as a whole. Obama at first seemed to be an exception. Taking office in January 2009, he had no choice. Two giant automakers—General Motors and Chrysler—were bankrupt or nearly so and in danger of having to shut most or all of their factories, which would almost certainly have plunged the nation into a recession. A three-person team appointed by the president brought the automakers through that crisis, mostly by arranging to have the federal government invest nearly $50 billion in GM stock and by forcing Chrysler to sell 58.5 percent of its equity to Fiat, the Italian automaker.[7] In hindsight, the auto bailout turned out to be the highpoint of the Obama administration's commitment to industrial policy, and may have won Ohio for him in the 2012 presidential election. But once past the crisis, the three team members one by one left the administration, and the position of assistant to the president for manufacturing policy ceased to exist, although Gene Sperling, as director of the National Economic Council, took manufacturing under his wing until he left the administration.[8] The future worried him: "a renaissance of U.S. manufacturing is not going to happen on its own, and its outcome is not predetermined. It requires long-term capital investments by both firms and governments," Sperling warned in a speech in July 2013 at a conference of manufacturing executives in Washington.[9]

After Sperling's tenure, the focus in Washington shifted to free trade agreements, and the view that they would contribute to higher, not lower, factory output in the United States—a shaky proposition at best, but one that the president and his advisers did not openly challenge. With Sperling's departure, the manufacturing portfolio fell to Ron Bloom, an alumnus of Harvard's Graduate School of Business, who had worked on Wall Street and also for the United Steelworkers (USW) before joining the Obama administration in 2009 as an assistant to the president for manufacturing policy. From the outset, Bloom muffled expectations, explaining readily to reporters that he worked from a basement office in the White House, with no staff beyond a secretary and an aide or two, and seldom met with President Obama. How could he implement industrial policy from such a sidelined post? he remarked to me and other reporters. Two and a half years later, Bloom returned quietly to Wall Street, as a vice chairman of Lazard Frères, the investment banking firm, and while the president replaced him, the new special assistant for manufacturing, Jason Miller, had little direct experience in the field, having worked mostly as a management consultant with the Boston Consulting Group.[10] Obama himself continued to make periodic visits to factories, and television newscasts showed footage of him in shirtsleeves and a hard hat, talking to blue-collar workers against the backdrop of factory assembly lines. But aside from the occasional optics, the administration's efforts to formulate an industrial policy dissolved once Sperling and Bloom were gone.

A federal industrial policy would have to formally acknowledge, for starters, that subsidies are already abundantly present in manufacturing, and essential to it. It would have to reject, once and for all, the misbegotten notion that government shouldn't pick winners—ignoring that state and local governments implicitly (and chaotically) pick winners every day in their endless bidding to induce a manufacturer to locate a factory in one city rather than another. A federal industrial policy would set goals for factory output in the entire United States and manipulate subsidies to achieve those goals, regardless of manufacturers' locations, even if that meant factories would concentrate in some cities rather than others. One such policy would focus on reducing the value of the dollar so that U.S.-manufactured merchandise could sell for less in the currencies of other countries, and as prices in those currencies fell, the demand overseas for exports from the United States presumably would rise. If that didn't happen in response to a weaker dollar, then federal industrial policy would require that the administration restrict imports until the annual trade deficit finally declined as domestic production rose. China—to cite the elephant in the room—might be required to buy more from the United States while a ceiling kicked in limiting what that country's factories could export to America. None of this would be easy to negotiate or enforce. The nation's swollen financial markets, for one, would push back, preferring a strong dollar to maintain the value of the securities traded on Wall Street. China, too, would push back, in support of its exports, which benefit from a strong dollar relative to its currency, the renminbi.

Still, whatever the challenges, and even the hardships, manufacturing more in America should be a national goal, and cutting back on the flows from abroad would be part of achieving that goal. Free trade would have to be curtailed, of course, forcing U.S.-based multinational manufacturers to open more factories in the United States and fewer abroad. The federal government might prod them into doing this by subsidizing exports and also by subsidizing consumers who purchase merchandise manufactured in the United States—a politically explosive "buy America" strategy that might work if retail prices somehow declined as this happened. The Roosevelt administration instituted a version of such a policy in the 1930s, convincing General Electric to mass produce low-priced appliances that were sold to consumers by the tens of thousands through the use of installment payments financed by the federal government.[11] The scheme worked, and modern consumer credit is a direct descendant.

On a related front, a newly enacted federal usury law, resurrecting ceilings that once were commonplace, would cap interest rates on loans, so that lenders could not charge anyone—individuals or businesses—more than, say, 8 or 9 percent annually for any borrowed money, including loans to finance investment and production as well as consumer purchases. Currently usury laws exist mostly at the state level, if they exist at all, and the ceilings they mandate have risen over the last thirty years.[12] The rise has come largely because borrowers in the hugely expanded financial markets earn higher profits trading securities than manufacturers do making physical products, and can afford therefore to pay higher interest rates on the money they borrow to finance their trades. That has to change, ideally through laws that limit the after-tax profits on financial transactions so that they are no greater than the after-tax profits from factory output. That symmetry was more or less the case in the first three decades after World War II, thanks to government regulations. Reviving such regulations should be a goal of the nation's political parties, or at least one of them. Far from being a goal, it wasn't even mentioned in the 2016 presidential election campaign.

Some of these steps would constitute a rollback to the policies of the Reagan administration, which took a more activist approach on trade issues than today's Republicans, and many current Democrats, for that matter. Reagan, for example, reacted to an overly strong dollar and a rising trade deficit by calling a meeting of the finance ministers and central bankers of the major U.S. trading partners and insisting on a devaluation of the dollar. The meeting took place on September 22, 1985, at the Plaza Hotel, just south of New York's Central Park. Japan, West Germany, Britain, and France were represented. They reluctantly agreed to a currency realignment that weakened the dollar, making exports from the United States less expensive in the currencies of these four nations.[13] Imports from these countries, by contrast, became more expensive to purchase in dollars, and by the late 1980s the trade deficit had begun to subside.

Of course, manufacturing in America was still a hugely important activity, accounting for 18 percent of the nation's GDP in those years. Corporate America had not yet put that many factories overseas. Domestic manufacturers still made in the United States most of what was sold in the domestic market, and foreign manufacturers joined them. When it came to "offshoring," companies such as Volkswagen, Honda, and Siemens established themselves early on in the United States—before American manufacturers began to spread factories en masse across the globe, and particularly in Asia. That happened just as China came on the scene in the late twentieth century with its rising flow of exports to the United States—operating not as a renegade but with the approval of the World Trade Organization, which China joined in December 2001. In accepting China, the WTO implicitly sanctioned the subsidies that flow to Chinese manufacturers, just as it had implicitly sanctioned the subsidies given to manufacturers in the United States. The WTO has rarely challenged the exports of either nation for being priced at less than "fair market value," although the subsidies available to manufacturers who export from the United States certainly mock calculations of that elusive standard.

A number of American manufacturers, for example, have erected factories on land given to them by municipal governments. Or they are granted multiyear tax exemptions. Or a state government reimburses a manufacturer for a portion of the wages paid to a factory's employees, without damaging the manufacturer's status in the free trade system. No one, for example, threw up trade barriers to Whirlpool after it opened a kitchen stove factory in Tulsa, Oklahoma, in 1996, although the Oklahoma government reimbursed Whirlpool 4.5 cents for every dollar paid in wages to the factory's 1,100 employees—a practice that continued into the twenty-first century. Other states adopted that tactic, and by the end of the century nearly thirty offered a similar subsidy to attract manufacturers.[14] Yet the WTO has never declared that manufacturers receiving such refunds, including Whirlpool, are ineligible for tariff-free trade. Free trade then has come to mean the selling of manufactured goods to customers in other countries, with the merchandise crossing borders unhindered by tariffs, but not free of subsidies—despite the fiction that subsidies don't play a significant role in global manufacturing.

Once that fiction can be put to rest, a more sensible, and certainly a more realistic substitute, managed trade, would recognize the presence of subsidies in nearly all merchandise manufactured in the industrialized nations, and in the-not-so industrialized as well. Given the huge flow of merchandise these subsidies help to make possible, candidates for public office, including those running for president, should include in their platforms their target for manufacturing output in the United States, and the subsidies they propose to achieve it. What should the target be? My answer is: enough to raise the output of the nation's factories to at least 19 percent of the gross domestic product. That is roughly equal to the sector's share in Japan, and 7 percentage points higher than manufacturing's actual contribution to U.S. GDP in 2015.[15] In pursuit of that 19 percent, companies such as Whirlpool, GM, and General Electric would be asked—even required, in exchange for subsidies—to make in the United States a portion of what they manufacture overseas. They would do so at the expense of free trade, and at the expense of the countries that now host them.[16] Americans (certainly those living in cities) would further benefit if a new federal industrial policy also insisted that a lopsided percentage of factories returning from abroad locate in urban areas and employ urban residents, even sweetening subsidies for those manufacturers who do so. Granted, government doesn't own the means of production, but it underwrites a large enough share of those means to have a deciding say in the geography of manufacturing.

If a manufacturer insists on offshoring, so be it, but not without first being required to consider a socially valuable alternative such as relocation to an urban neighborhood that needs the jobs and pay-checks. The subsidies that manufacturers receive should require no less, particularly if they are channeled through Washington as part of a federal industrial policy. Hopefully, millions of voters would line up in support, once the pros and cons were publicly—and repeatedly—explained. In the 2016 election campaign, they weren't.

On another level, there is little public awareness of the damaging trade-offs when cities such as Cincinnati, Cleveland, Baltimore, New York, Los Angeles, and St. Louis spend huge sums to subsidize the construction of sports stadiums or expensive apartment complexes or medical centers and research institutes, or all of these, rather than factories.[17] Again, high school–educated men and women are shortchanged. Instead of transitioning to relatively well-paying assembly line jobs in factories, they transition to numerous jobs outside manufacturing that rarely pay as well, given the more limited value added generated in most other commercial activity. By their nature, factories not only generate enough value added to fund higher wage levels but enough cohesion among a factory's workers (standing side by side on assembly lines) to pry away a large enough share of that value added to fund generous wages. In the United States, unions have been and continue to be agents in cementing this cohesion and the bargaining power it makes possible. In manufacturing, they should also be thought of as agents in the distribution of the value added that subsidies, funded by taxpayers, help to make possible.

Maybe that will happen. Or maybe unions won't ever regain their once considerable bargaining power in manufacturing—before the nation's factory owners moved a significant portion of their production overseas, starting in the 1980s, in part to get away from unions. And while unions have certainly protested this migration, they have failed to raise the subsidy issue, failed to assert that manufacturers are indebted to those who provide subsidies (that is, millions of taxpayers, including union members), and therefore should not be free to offshore without public consent in some form. Nor should they be free to shift production to another city within the United States without public approval. Or to move factories away from urban neighborhoods without the public having a say in the matter. Or to take any step, for that matter, that would be disruptive for the taxpaying public, which feeds them subsidies.

Harley-Davidson, the motorcycle manufacturer, for example, publicly declared in 2010 that it would move some factory operations from Milwaukee, where it is headquartered, to a lower-wage city such as Stillwater, Oklahoma, or Kansas City, Missouri, if its hourly workers in Milwaukee failed to accept certain concessions set forth in a proposed new contract with the USW.[18] One provision would permit Harley-Davidson's management to avoid overtime pay at its Milwaukee factory by bringing in up to 250 "temps"—nearly one-third of the regular workforce—to handle surges in demand. The temps would receive $18.50 an hour, compared with the $25.00 or more that regular employees earned.[19] In the end, the regulars, represented by the USW, gave in and ratified the contract, fearful they might lose their jobs altogether if Harley-Davidson carried out its threat to relocate. The city's taxpayers, however, were given no say in the matter—no opportunity to bat down Harley's threat—although their taxes helped to subsidize the company's operation in Milwaukee. "Management clearly has the upper hand in negotiations because of the employment situation," Tom Barrett, the Democratic mayor of Milwaukee, told me during an interview at City Hall.[20] At the time I failed to challenge his assertion from the point of view of the city's residents, whose taxes should have given them a right to amend Harley's plan, and even to veto it by withholding subsidies from the company. Because the subsidies went unrecognized, the taxpayers who provided them lost their leverage. And what happened in Milwaukee happens repeatedly across the country, when companies receiving subsidies relocate, leaving in the lurch the taxpayers who had funded their subsidies in one form or another.

For GE's factory complex in Louisville's Appliance Park, the subsidy is quite direct. The city collects a wage tax from everyone employed in Louisville. Each employer, including GE, withholds the tax, which comes to 2 percent of an employee's earnings, and delivers the money to the city. In GE's case, however, the city became concerned that the company might move a factory or two away from Louisville. So it decided in 2011 that henceforth it would rebate to GE the wage tax the company collected from its 2,300 employees—in effect lowering GE's wage cost by that percentage, a significant subsidy aimed at keeping the factory in place. The International Union of Electrical Workers, representing the employees, agreed to the arrangement, its hope being that GE would not shrink its Appliance Park operation any more than it already had—from seventeen thousand in the 1970s. Five years later, GE still employed 2,300 people in Appliance Park, nearly all of them in the manufacture of refrigerators.

As a *New York Times* reporter, I watched the damage unfold on visits to factory towns in the 1980s and 1990s—among them New Britain, Connecticut, home of The Stanley Works, a leading manufacturer of wrenches, screwdrivers, pliers, saws, and other hand tools; and Wooster, Ohio, dominated then by Rubbermaid, which made such items as dustpans, wastebaskets, and kitchenware, most of it molded from plastic or rubber. Like so many manufacturers, both companies had concentrated their production in these cities of their birth. Subsidies targeted at keeping factories in such cities at existing wage levels would have constituted an enlightened and merciful industrial policy, but neither the Democrats nor the Republicans, locally or nationally, thought in those terms. Nor did the unions, despite the damage inflicted on their members.

The Stanley Works and Rubbermaid eventually moved most of their production to sites in the South and West, where subsidies were abundant and unemployment rates high enough for workers to jump at the relatively modest wages the two companies offered in their new locations. In the process, they shook off the unions that had represented their workers in the Northeast and Midwest. That was certainly a priority for Richard H. Ayers, who became chairman and CEO of The Stanley Works in 1989 and over the next few years presided over the migration of Stanley's factory production to cities with weaker unions or none at all. He was, of course, not alone; many manufacturers did the same. And as manufacturing jobs disappeared from their old locations in the 1980s and 1990s, union power inevitably declined and the upward pressure on wages largely dissolved, at least for younger workers, who were willing to accept smaller annual wage increases than the previous generation. The alternative, after all, was even lower pay in occupations outside manufacturing.

Manufacturers in the United States have collected in recent years roughly forty cents in subsidies or public money for every two dollars in new value that they and their employees generate by converting materials and components into finished products. More than one-third of that forty cents flows from the Department of Defense in payments for the manufacture of weapons and other ordnance delivered to the armed forces—or from state, county, and local governments in payment for all the factory-made merchandise they purchase. A midsize city purchases police cars, sanitation trucks, uniforms, office furniture, fire engines, tools, snowplows, lawn mowers, and concrete and steel for the construction of municipal buildings, public schools, roads, and bridges—not to mention computers and electronic equipment. "Buy America" clauses in many of the purchase contracts require that as many items as possible of this long list are made in factories in the United States.

Municipal and state subsidies are used, as we saw in chapter 3, to lure manufacturers to new locations. In a better world, federal subsidies would encourage manufacturers to stay put, particularly in cities, shunning the factory migrations that reduce blue-collar incomes and family well-being in the left-behind cities. The citizens of Newton, Iowa, went through this experience rather dramatically in the years when I periodically visited that city in the first decade of the twenty-first century. The big employer, Maytag, made washing machines there, in a sprawling factory on the edge of town, and the company also had its headquarters in Newton, in a beige-colored granite-like office building downtown. More than two thousand people worked at the two locations, drawn from the town's 15,500 residents and from the surrounding countryside. Then in 2006, Whirlpool purchased Maytag, closing both buildings and laying off everyone.[21] Whirlpool continued to make some Maytag machines, or at least machines with a Maytag label, but not in Iowa. They were manufactured instead at Whirlpool factories in Clyde, Ohio, and Monterrey, Mexico. Newton never replaced the wages or the tax revenue that Maytag had generated as a stand-alone corporation. The federal government might have blocked the merger, citing the public subsidies that both companies received as a justification for its intervention, not to mention the well-paying unionized jobs that would—and did—disappear, after Whirlpool bought Maytag. But absent an industrial policy authorized by Congress—one that would seek to increase factory output and employment within the United States, and particularly in cities—the federal government had no mandate to intervene.[22]

U.S. manufacturers receive subsidies in a variety of forms. They kick in most visibly as outlays for the construction and maintenance of public infrastructure: that is, for the roads, sewers, airports, railroads, canals, river and harbor facilities, computer and telephone networks, high-voltage power lines, and the water ducts that people need in their daily lives, and that manufacturers must also have to operate a factory. For lack of sophisticated infrastructure, third-world countries can't support factories of great consequence while first-world countries spend huge sums to do so, although in the United States the vast infrastructure that still sustains our industrial might has deteriorated so much that nearly $4 trillion dollars would have to be spent on maintenance to restore its efficiency.[23] In addition, government builds and operates huge hydroelectric projects and nuclear reactors that supply power in abundance to factories as well as to homes, offices, and other commercial buildings.[24] Revere Copper Products in Rome, New York, is a vivid example of public infrastructure performing in the service of manufacturing.[25] Revere has regularly purchased the electricity it needs to produce its copper from the State of New York. The electricity is supplied by the New York State Power Authority, which has sold it to Revere at a deep discount—in effect, a state subsidy large enough to make Revere marginally profitable in the spring of 2012, when I visited Rome, spending an evening and a day with Brian O'Shaughnessy, then Revere's chairman.

O'Shaughnessy had been hired in the late 1980s to run the company after Michael Milken, the corporate raider, acquired Revere in a leveraged buyout, one of the dozens of such transactions that, in recent years, transferred ownership of between three and five hundred manufacturing operations annually to private equity firms.[26] O'Shaughnessy eventually bought Revere in a leveraged buyout of his own. By the time of my visit, the state subsidy accounted for half of Revere's annual profit, according to O'Shaughnessy. That's what kept his factory in the state, he insisted, along with its 360 workers. "The only manufacturers in America who go without government support are those whose markets are so insignificant that they are not noticed," O'Shaughnessy said.[27]

That's not many. Certainly not the numerous small manufacturers who have settled at the old Brooklyn Navy Yard, a three hundred–acre site on the East River purchased by New York City and converted mostly into an industrial park, with roads wide enough to accommodate tractor-trailer trucks that transport merchandise made at factories in the park. The city has kept rents, and also municipal taxes, well below the cost of similar factory sites elsewhere in Brooklyn. Most of the manufacturers are small, such as Crye Precision, which employed 175 people in the manufacture of military-style backpacks, pouches, and body armor when I visited in the spring of 2015. In one large and well-lit hall, several dozen Chinese-American women worked diligently at sewing machines. They were recent immigrants living in Brooklyn neighborhoods near the factory and they looked up silently as I walked through the hall on a tour of the factory. They did not yet speak much English, Caleb Crye, the thirty-eight-year-old chief executive, explained. On another front, the rent he paid in 2015 to house his operation at the old Navy yard—less than fifteen dollars per square foot—was unusually low for prime New York City real estate, but it was a rent that helped to make manufacturing in New York viable. "We are in a bit of a sweet spot," Crye said.

For the nation, subsidies for manufacturers have come to roughly $80 billion a year in the second decade of the twenty-first century, plus—and it's a big plus—the $700 billion or so that the federal government spends annually to procure from American manufacturers weapons and other materiel for the armed forces.[28] The total of $780 billion helps to pay the wages and benefits of factory workers, to purchase land on which to locate a factory, to lower the cost of constructing a new factory or expanding an existing one, to reduce the cost of electric power and natural gas, to support worker training, to build and maintain roads and rail spurs, to dredge river channels, to maintain canals and harbors and all the other transportation infrastructure that factories need, and to subsidize daily production costs.

Americans by the tens of millions simply don't notice these supplements to private investment or they take them for granted, seldom thinking of them as industrial subsidies. That's because we so often benefit as well from the enhanced transportation and from the plentiful supply of water and electricity in our daily lives.[29] We regularly approve bond issues to build these facilities and to upgrade them periodically, and more often than not we approve of new taxes to pay down the bonds. Certainly we don't very often balk or complain, by arguing at a public hearing or in a petition, for example, that the various public works provide huge benefits to local factories, which therefore should pay a disproportionately large share of their costs. If anything, we sometimes permit factory owners to forgo paying even a reasonable share, on the ground they are big employers in their communities and, in exchange, deserve tax breaks. The relationship is symbiotic. Moreover, the amounts spent by government at the local, state, and federal levels on all manner of manufactured supplies made in the United States add to the evidence that more than 20 percent of the nation's factory output is purchased directly with public money.[30] That makes government, including the military, the biggest single consumer of what comes out of the nation's factories.

In addition, the so-called location wars contribute heavily to the flow of public money to companies that are privately or shareholder owned. Rather than constructing a new factory or an office tower or a research center with their own funds, many manufacturers organize informal auctions in which they encourage towns, cities, and states to bid for their presence, which the latter regularly do. Often a manufacturer, seeking the biggest subsidy package, subcontracts such an auction to specialists, who are usually employed by "site selection" companies. Although these bidding wars are not limited to manufacturers, the latter are big players, avidly sought after by communities as significant sources of blue-collar jobs. Governments provide funding for these auctions in the form of cash grants, tax reductions, free land on which to build a new factory, and municipal bond issues floated to pay for the construction of a factory building or for the expansion of an existing one. Public funds also subsidize the construction of access roads and railroad links. Furthermore, they pay for the installation of electric power generators and for worker training, and in some cases—such as the GE facility in Louisville, Kentucky—they lower a company's net wage cost.

GE's Louisville rebate, of course, is industrial policy—if shortsighted industrial policy. Subsidizing a company in any form so that it will keep a factory in one community rather than moving it to another, lured in part by a better subsidy, has become a greater goal than using subsidies to increase factory output in both communities and in the nation as a whole. Military spending is similarly shortsighted, if a principal goal is to multiply factory output in the United States as much as possible. On one level, making a tank for the U.S. Army or an over-the-highway tractor-trailer for commercial use adds indistinguishably to factory output. But a tank is useful only in a military action while a tractor-trailer hauls merchandise and materials repeatedly to all sorts of destinations—and some of the materials, once delivered, become components in additional factory output. The multiplier effect from the manufacture of civilian goods such as tractor-trailers is consequently greater, which suggests that federal industrial policy should try to skew factories toward the production of civilian merchandise and away from weapons.

Unfortunately, weapons production has become a goal in itself—a subsidy run amok, so to speak. We don't say that. We argue instead that the United States, Russia, and China are rival powers, which they are, and the United States therefore must maintain a considerable arsenal to prevent the two others from expanding their political and commercial influence, not to mention their physical presence, in such places as Ukraine and the South China Sea. These international power struggles provide the ostensible justification for spending huge amounts each year to manufacture weapons. But manufacturers stick tenaciously to weapons production in peacetime as well, and they resisted in 1991 when the administration of George H.W. Bush attempted a large-scale conversion from military to civilian production—the only such attempt since the Korean War in the early 1950s.

Their leader in this endeavor was William A. Anders, chairman and chief executive of General Dynamics, a giant manufacturer then of M1 Abrams tanks, jet fighter planes, and nuclear submarines, and still a major weapons maker. In a speech in the fall of 1991 Anders keynoted the resistance of weapons manufacturers to the Bush administration's proposed policy.[31] The production of civilian merchandise involves techniques different from those used in the production of weapons, he said—techniques that have to be learned, and which require changing the way the company works. Given these drawbacks, General Dynamics would continue to manufacture weapons, but fewer of them, if the administration insisted on conversion. Specifically, it would shrink production capacity rather than convert any of it to the manufacture of civilian merchandise.[32] And that it did, eliminating nearly seventeen thousand of its ninety thousand employees. It also repurchased shares, spending nearly $1 billion to buy back 30 percent of its outstanding stock.[33] The message in this tactic: Better to be a smaller weapons manufacturer than to convert to less profitable lines of business.

But should General Dynamics have had that option? Should any weapons manufacturer have the right to resist civilian conversion when its sales revenue and profits come mainly from government spending—in essence, from a prolonged subsidy? General Dynamics, for example, might have converted to the production of iron and steel pipes large enough in diameter to carry water under urban streets. Those pipes might have replaced worn-out ones installed decades ago in numerous U.S. towns and cities. And government would have purchased the pipes, just as it purchased and still purchases the weapons, if not at the federal level, then at the state or municipal level. Since the projected profit from the production of civilian merchandise, any civilian merchandise, would have been less, General Dynamics chose to downsize instead. In doing so, it continued to manufacture submarines and other state-of-the-art warships—fewer of them, but even so working for the Navy remained a more profitable activity than the production of civilian vessels would have been. As of 2014, General Dynamics was the nation's fifth-largest weapons contractor, with $18 billion in sales to the

Department of Defense, or 58 percent of its total annual revenue, which had also declined.[34]

The significant role that subsidies play in manufacturing is a difficult admission for the U.S. government and its citizens to make. What goes unsaid is that no one anywhere in the world makes steel or autos or shoes or virtually anything else in a factory without subsidies. That's the nature of manufacturing in any society, and now that the twentieth century's ideological struggles are over, we can get on with the business of raising factory output in the United States to a share of the economy consistent with that of a powerful industrial nation. The false premise that manufacturing is a free-market activity—that subsidies don't exist or are inconsequential—should finally be put to rest.

5

Offshoring and How It Could Be Reversed: The Challenges

Cross the border into Mexico from Laredo or El Paso or Nogales and drive south on the multilane highways that connect northern Mexico to the United States. If you leave after breakfast, by lunchtime the auto factories will begin to appear, like emplacements in a Maginot Line that stretches from Hermosillo in the northwest through Chihuahua on the central plateau to Monterrey in the northeast. The cars, trucks, and SUVs assembled in these factories are loaded onto tractor-trailers and taken north to the border cities, en route to dealerships in numerous American communities. Or they don't go north to the United States. A significant number move southeast, by tractor-trailer or freight train, to Tampico and other Mexican ports, for export to Europe and South America.

The multinational corporations that manufacture these vehicles in northern Mexico also operate most of the auto factories in the United States: General Motors, Ford, Chrysler, Toyota, Honda, Nissan, Hyundai, Volkswagen. They could make in the United States the vehicles they manufacture instead in northern Mexico, jacking up output and employment north of the border. But why should they? Thanks to the North American Free Trade Agreement (NAFTA), the array of cars and light trucks manufactured in Mexico cross the border into the United States as easily as those made in Michigan cross state lines into Indiana and Ohio, or into any other state. And there is another huge advantage—for the manufacturers: Mexico has free trade agreements with forty-five nations, while the United States has them with only twenty. That makes Mexico a better platform than the United States from which to export manufactured goods, tariff free. This web of agreements should be every factory worker's nightmare, given how easily a factory can be closed in the United States and reopened in Mexico more lucratively, or closed in Europe and Japan and reopened in Mexico, also more lucratively. Mexico's advantages as an export platform help to explain why factory output in the United States has failed to rise significantly in recent decades. Yet the two mainstream American political parties and their leaders—in their platforms and speeches—have consistently failed to confront such plain-as-day obstacles to a resurgence of domestic U.S. manufacturing. The needle finally moved in the 2016 presidential election campaign, when the two populist insurgents—Donald Trump in the Republican camp and Bernie Sanders among the Democrats—targeted free trade agreements as the drains on domestic manufacturing they actually have been in NAFTA's case and are likely to be if the Trans Pacific Partnership (TPP) were to become law despite Trump's opposition.[1]

Perhaps manufacturing's contributions to the American economy and to employment are no longer large enough, or seem no longer large enough, to pressure the mainstream media into beating the drums against free trade agreements, or into examining the drag they exert on domestic manufacturing. After all, the multinational corporations that account for most of the nation's factory output have a stake in agreements that allow them to put factories so easily in other countries, as the automakers have done in northern Mexico, and also in China. Take GM, which sold 3.5 million vehicles in China in 2015. Its Chinese factories—operated in partnership with a Chinese company, as required by the Chinese government— contributed handsomely to the total of 24.5 million vehicles manufactured annually in that nation. By 2015, in fact, China produced more vehicles each year than any other nation.[2] If even 3 million of them—those made by General Motors—had been manufactured in the United States and exported to China, the additional output would have increased vehicle production in GM's home country by 12 percent, which would have raised overall U.S. economic growth significantly. Continuing this fantasy, if other industries that have offshored large portions of their factory production—from furniture-making to clothing to lightbulbs to dinnerware to clocks to semi-conductors to textiles to toys to glass to construction equipment and many, many other goods—were to bring that production home, economic growth in the United States would gradually rise. And in a decade or two, America would be restored as a manufacturing giant on par with its status in the 1960s—and on par with China's current status.

That isn't going to happen, and America's days as the world leader in manufacturing aren't likely to return. A vigorous industrial policy would slow the decline, by withholding subsidies from Boeing, for example, until it agreed to purchase all or nearly all the parts and components of its airliners from suppliers whose factories were located in the United States. Stronger unions, persistently opposed to offshoring, would also slow the process, particularly if they could somehow regain the broad public support that unions enjoyed in the immediate postwar decades, when one-third of the workforce was unionized, and millions of Americans, including me, felt obliged to purchase merchandise that had been made by these workers. In the mid-1970s, for example, I acquired a gray Ford sedan rather than a similar-in-size but slightly less expensive Japanese car, although the imported Japanese vehicle would have been more reliable, according to *Consumer Reports*. The Ford, however, carried a sticker in the window declaring that it had been assembled in Michigan by members of the United Auto Workers union. That counted in those days.

Above all, federal government subsidies would have to be aimed at increasing the nation's factory output across the spectrum, from low-tech to high-tech products, and in cities as well as in suburbs and rural areas. There would be no more regional competitions in which one city outbids another (with taxpayer money) to persuade a manufacturer to locate a factory in, say, Kansas City rather than York, Pennsylvania, while closing one in Battle Creek, Michigan, a zero-sum game for the nation as a whole. In exchange for federal permission to construct a factory in a different city, or to expand an existing one, the manufacturer would have to agree to increase its overall factory output in the United States, even "reshoring" some production from abroad to meet a federally specified requirement. That would be the opposite of the current practice, in which vehicles are funneled to the United States from the auto factories strung across northern Mexico, to cite again that outrageous example. GM in China is another. In that case, the auto giant would be required to export from factories within the United States 2 million or so of the 3.5 million vehicles that it manufactured in China in 2015, which would constitute a massive reshoring.

Could all this happen? I don't see how, in a nation whose political parties have failed to insist on such specific goals, and whose biggest manufacturers produce so much in factories overseas. If they do someday change their ways and come home, or even try to return to the United States, the Chinese would undoubtedly raise Cain. The American gain would be, in large measure, China's lost production. To keep going forward, a new policy—managed trade in place of free trade—would have to emerge, one that augments domestic factory output by requiring U.S.-headquartered multinational manufacturers to reshore a significant share of their overseas output. There would have to be a sort of mass migration back to the United States from various parts of the world, including some or all of the American-owned auto factories in northern Mexico, and many factories in Asia. Could all this happen? The answer is no; it's too late.

What might still have been possible in the 1990s, and perhaps even in the earliest years of the current century, no longer is possible, in large part because Americans are no longer the world's only robust consumers. In Europe and Asia, and also in South America and the Middle East, consumption is rising at a faster rate (most of the time) than in the United States, and factory production has shifted accordingly. The shift is distressing for millions of high school–educated hourly workers in the United States who once staffed the missing factories. It is also distressing for their children, who might have had relatively well-paying factory jobs, if only those jobs had not disappeared. Donald Trump became the Republican presidential candidate in 2016 in part by fanning this distress with his dangerous promise to "make America great again." He won that election, voted into office by tens of thousands of men and women who see themselves as damaged wage earners—superseded people—and who want redress. Absent more factories and many more factory jobs, they aren't likely to get it. Manufacturing in America is that important.

Sidestepping reality, we spotlight the reshoring of factory production that has gone abroad, and declare that it's the beginning of a much broader migration. The reshoring, however, turns out to be small potatoes. The relatively few companies that have brought production home have done so because all or nearly all of their customers are in the United States, and serving them from faraway factories saved no money, it turned out. The spotlight instead should be on the reluctance of manufacturers to bring factories home when those factories supply merchandise purchased mainly by people in the factories' host countries. GM's managers, for example, have no stake in reshoring factories from China that generate the sale of so many GM vehicles sold in that nation. The only way out of this impasse is for the Chinese and the American governments to somehow negotiate an agreement that returns some GM production to the United States, with GM then exporting an agreed-upon number of vehicles to China—a difficult negotiation at best. The outcome would be managed trade. In its absence, is it any wonder that reshoring happens infrequently?

It is, in fact, a very small course correction, based on a belated realization that putting factories overseas, particularly in Asia, to manufacture merchandise entirely for American consumption, has not paid off as expected. It's one thing to manufacture just across the border in northern Mexico and quite another to do it in a factory across an ocean as wide as the Pacific. Sure, there were savings in wages, in lax regulations, in rent-free factories, in less militant workers, and so on, but these were offset by difficulties in managing distant operations from offices in the United States, as well as in time lost while shipping merchandise back home. The prolonged shipping time represents in effect a huge investment tied up in unsold inventory warehoused at sea.

Dealing with these obstacles, some companies have calculated, in hindsight, the true cost of offshoring, and have concluded that they could save money by returning production to the United States. That hasn't been the case for multinationals such as GM, whose factories in Asia marched, and still march, to a different dynamic, turning out vehicles for sale overseas as well as in the United States. But it has proven true for many small manufacturers whose customers were all back in America—companies such as Accu-Rounds, which machines metal parts to precise dimensions, and Bailey Hydropower, which makes hydraulic cylinders. AccuRounds transferred production to its factory in Avon, Massachusetts, from China and Europe, and Bailey to a factory in West Knoxville, Tennessee, from Chennai, India.[3] AccuRounds cited faster delivery to customers, rising wages abroad, and concessions from its employees in Avon as among its reasons for reshoring, while Hydraulic Cylinders listed fewer quality problems than in China, as well as faster delivery.[4]

All this shows up on the website of the Reshoring Initiative, an advocacy organization headquartered in Chicago that tracks the returnees as well as the savings they achieve by reshoring some or all of their production.[5] The website lists some 1,300 companies, including a few big ones, such as General Electric, that have reshored at least some factory production from 2010 through mid-2016. Included in the list are manufacturers who decided against putting factories overseas in the first place after considering the pros and cons. Even so, the number of jobs saved in the United States or brought home from abroad—a total of 265,000 as of July 2016—is alarmingly small.[6] The average for these five and a half years is just 4,015 a month, a total almost unnoticeable in a nation that regularly generates, or sheds, more than 200,000 jobs a month.

More manufacturing within the United States would lift morale, in part by making manual labor a more respected activity. The trade deficit would also shrink if multinational giants such as GM, GE, and a host of others brought home chunks of their overseas production. But reshoring as it is actually practiced has not added up to much and is unlikely to do so despite the publicity it generates, as reflected in the rise of the Reshoring Initiative and the overhyped verb *to reshore*. If manufacturing is the foundation of a nation's power—and it is—then the United States is gradually sinking to the role of a powerful nation among other powerful nations. And offshoring—permanent offshoring—is an agent in this process.

Permanent offshoring, which greatly outstrips reshoring, pays off if a significant portion of a manufacturer's customers live nearby, as many increasingly do in Asia, India, the Middle East, and Africa, where employment, wages, and purchasing power have risen for millions of families. Offshoring also pays off if a foreign government offers special deals, as China does for GM and other multinationals. It can also be the more profitable option if the host government, like Mexico's, has more free trade agreements than the United States, and thus can offer a better export platform. "Reshoring only really relates to products that are to be sold in the U.S. market," according to Harry Moser, an engineer educated at MIT and a former manufacturing executive who has worked out a formula for comparing the costs of operating a factory overseas versus operating the same factory in the United States (the formula is posted on the website of the Reshoring Initiative, which Moser founded). Actual production and transportation costs in one nation versus another are the key issues in each of the Reshoring Initiative's case studies, but subsidies have also played a role in the reshoring process as municipal and state governments bid against each other to persuade a returning manufacturer to locate in one community rather than another. This competition has in turn contributed to the rise of numerous economic development officials in cities and counties across the United States who organize the bidding to lure returnees to their communities. What do they offer? "Typically, in this bidding, a company is looking for tax abatements to defer what they would otherwise have to pay up front in taxes or in the first few years," said Greg Wathen, the energetic chief of the Economic Development Coalition of Southwest Indiana, a public agency headquartered in Evanston.

But Wathen, a participant in this bidding, recognized a predicament. I first met him at a reshoring conference in Cleveland in March of 2013. From speeches at that conference, as well as from remarks made at the various breakout sessions, it was clear that the American-owned companies that had reshored, or were thinking of doing so, were too few in number—and often too small—to generate much of a manufacturing revival. For example, Aviator Sunglasses returned just *fifteen* jobs from Asia to its operation in Southbridge, Massachusetts, listing the eyeglasses brand's favorable public image as a reason to step up production in the United States—and also the lure of a state government subsidy in Massachusetts.[7] Somewhat more impressively, DeWalt Power Tools, a subsidiary of Stanley Black & Decker, expanded a factory in Charlotte, North Carolina, adding 250 jobs, because of what the company described as a consumer preference "for American-made power tools," particularly among workers who used the tools.[8] In DeWalt's case, the new policy constituted an about-face more than a decade after the company had moved all of its tool production to China and Mexico. Like AccuRounds and Bailey Hydropower, however, neither of these companies is large enough to reverse manufacturing's declining contribution to the American economy.

While Wathen beats the bushes for American companies that might reshore, his main task is to convince manufacturers, whatever their nationality, to locate factories in southwestern Indiana, and if that means wooing and winning a foreign-owned manufacturer, that's fine. Regardless of a factory's ownership, value added in the United States goes up as it turns parts and materials into finished products. Wathen's argument is that a factory in southwestern Indiana has fairly rapid access to consumers in the middle of the country as well as a plentiful supply of highly skilled unemployed engineers and technicians. In the summer and fall of 2015, for example, a Chinese company, Haier Group, which manufactures more household appliances than any other company in the world, opened a tech center in Evansville, wooed there by Wathen. It was the company's first tech center in the United States. It occupied a shuttered Coca Cola bottling plant, and Haier quickly hired three hundred engineers, tapping into "the talent left behind by Whirlpool," as Wathen put it, when Whirlpool closed a product design center in 2014.[9] At the same time, Haier announced an expansion of its appliance factory in Camden, South Carolina.

So the factory output of a Chinese multinational—in this case, Haier—expands in the United States in the same way that GM's factory output expands in China. Enlightened industrial policy would dictate that Haier and GM export from their home countries rather than offshore production—in the process strengthening another nation's economy rather than their own. True, Haier's home country, China, isn't as hard-pressed as GM's for more factory output—or as committed as the United States is to free trade agreements that drain away production so easily, sometimes no further than northern Mexico, a morning's drive from the border.

Raising factory output within the United States by 6 or 7 percentage points, to between 17 and 20 percent of GDP, a respectable level for an industrial nation, should have been a billboard issue in the 2016 presidential campaign. The issue was represented, indirectly, in the broad support for Donald Trump, whose followers included ex–factory workers, or men and women who might have worked in factories had the jobs existed, but have ended up instead in lower-paying work. The candidates for president and those farther down the ballot, or at least some of them, should have argued vigorously that no other industry generates enough value added to support a wage of twenty dollars an hour or more for tens of thousands of semiskilled, high school–educated assembly line workers. No one pushed that point in support of domestic manufacturing, or not vigorously. The pull overseas in the second decade of the twenty-first century has been too strong, and the concepts that our political and business elites embody and salute in our trade agreements seem too ingrained to return industrial production and well-paying factory jobs en masse to the United States.

President Obama tried to buck the exodus in the early years of his administration by giving special emphasis to manufacturing. The auto industry bailout started just weeks after his inauguration on January 20, 2009. And two years later, Obama created the Office of Manufacturing Policy, giving cabinet-level attention to manufacturing's dwindling share of the U.S. economy. But in 2013 that office dissolved, although one of its three initial leaders, Ron Bloom, stayed on for a while as assistant to the president for manufacturing policy—a vestige of the administration's initial high-profile concern about manufacturing. "Maybe because of the auto bailout and the mood it created," Bloom told me in 2015, recalling events in the early years of the Obama administration, "there was a little bit of a boomlet in public concern about the importance of manufacturing, and I think it coincided with my having the job."[10]

In the end, as the surviving advocate for manufacturing within the White House, Bloom's influence dwindled. "I never really got significant access to China policy, which is part of the reason I left the administration, because if you are not playing in China policy, you are not doing a lot for manufacturing," Bloom told me, "and the White House chose not to insist that manufacturing get an explicit seat at the China table. . . . The argument was that manufacturing is dying anyway; let it go."[11]

Manufacturing is not dying, of course. Its output in the United States rises almost every year, although more slowly than output in other sectors of the economy.[12] As a result, it shrinks as a share of the total economy, and that shrinkage finally triggered the "let it go" attitude that Bloom encountered in the administration.[13] Manufacturers themselves could have insisted that the administration pay more attention, but the dominant ones are multinational corporations, and like the auto companies in northern Mexico or GM in China, they maintain large shares of their production overseas. Their loyalties are divided. Organized labor could have raised a hue and cry, but with factory employment in the United States—particularly blue-collar employment—having fallen off a cliff since 1979, their stake in the welfare of factory workers has declined.[14] In addition, the migration of factories away from cities dispersed factory employment, diluting the bargaining leverage that workers once possessed.

Without a vigorous national industrial policy, there is little hope—probably no hope—of fixing these problems. Reshoring won't do it. Not enough manufacturers would bring production home. Canceling free trade agreements would help. But as the U.S. auto factories in northern Mexico illustrate, persuading companies to shut factories abroad and reopen them in the United States would involve a huge expense, one that the federal government would almost certainly have to subsidize, assuming the companies would agree to come home, and in doing so endanger their access to rich foreign markets, not to mention the subsidies that foreign governments offer.

More to the point, the American public no longer pressures U.S. manufacturers to put the United States first in locating their factories, having gradually acquiesced to offshoring. Yet the outburst of support for Trump and Sanders suggests that what has passed for acquiescence has only hidden simmering resentment over the disappearance of too many well-paying jobs. I ran across evidence of this during periodic reporting trips to the Midwest, including one in the summer of 2006 to Rock Falls, Illinois, where I spent the better part of a summer afternoon at the home of Alan Beggerow, a laid-off steelworker, sitting on his unscreened front porch, discussing his predicament.

Beggerow, who was then forty-eight, wanted to tell his story to a *New York Times* reporter. He wanted to present himself to the world as an example of a man who had once been well paid and refused to take a job that he considered beneath him, even if that meant dropping out of paid employment. After the layoff, he had taught math and how to read blueprints at a community college, although he was never a college student himself, having ended his formal education with a high school diploma. When I met him, he was spending his days at home, playing the piano, reading history and biography, and writing western potboilers in the Louis L'Amour style—all activities once relegated to spare time. When we reconnected by phone a decade later, he told me he had self-published fifteen books, many of them available on Amazon.[15] "Several are on classical music," he said, explaining that he had taken piano lessons for ten years, starting when he was twenty-five.

Beggerow, a powerfully built six-footer, had earned twenty-five dollars an hour for a forty-five-hour week at the Northwestern Steel and Wire Company in Sterling, Illinois, not far from his home in Rock Falls. When we reconnected, his income had dwindled, at age sixty-three, to $2,900 a month in federally subsidized pensions, with a big chunk of that amount in the form of disability pay after neck surgery to correct nerve damage. Along the way, his wife had died, and he had remarried, sold his home, and purchased a less expensive one in Sterling. His new wife, however, had lost her job as a teacher of immigrants' children, when the grant that funded the program in which she taught ran out. "You can say she's between jobs," he said.[16]

Beggerow describes himself as a lifelong Democrat who voted for Bill Clinton twice but blames him for negotiating NAFTA, which, in Beggerow's view, prompted manufacturers to shift a lot of factory production to Mexico, depriving workers like himself of jobs. That blame extended to Hillary Clinton in 2016. "I'm a big Bernie Sanders supporter; I'm with him all the way," Beggerow said, arguing (six months before the election) that Sanders—and also Trump—would be more likely than Clinton to cancel NAFTA and in doing so force at least some manufacturers to reshore their factories. All during his working life, and then in retirement, Beggerow had counted on the United Steelworkers to lift his wages and regulate his working days through the contracts the union negotiated. Even in retirement he remained committed to unions, although in his view those representing factory workers have gradually muted their resistance to trade agreements such as NAFTA and to offshoring in general. What was still an emotional political issue during the Clinton and Bush administrations, as Beggerow recalls, no longer was by Obama's last year in office. And then Sanders and Trump reshaped the 2016 election. They denounced NAFTA and TPP as damaging to American workers, though each for a different reason. But both essentially tapped into the same long-simmering discontent shared by high school–educated men and women, mostly white, who were losing ground because their wage increases, if any, had failed to keep pace with or exceed the annual rate of inflation. Their purchasing power had steadily declined, and the unions representing them had failed to negotiate the tough wage agreements that had been commonplace in the heyday of American manufacturing, agreements that gave hourly workers a significant share of the value added generated through factory production.

So blue-collar workers turned in particular to Trump, who blamed illegal immigrants (and nonwhites in general), and promised to build a wall along the Mexican border that would prevent Hispanics from entering the country illegally, while Muslims would be stopped at airports and other entry points. With the flow from abroad restricted, more jobs would open up for Americans—particularly white Americans—and wages would rise as employers competed to hire them—or so Trump suggested. *Voilà!* America would be great again! For those workers who disagreed with Trump's rhetoric, or were repelled by it, there was Sanders, who promised free national health care and other generous federal programs to offset workers' lost income.

What's most striking in the rise of Trump and Sanders is that their candidacies were made possible, and plausible, by the relentless downward pressure on factory output and employment: not just lost jobs that paid well, but the mountain of imports that have supplanted U.S. output, and the free trade agreements such as NAFTA that have kept the imports flowing. The glass that went into the new World Trade Center in lower Manhattan, to cite a very notable example, came mostly from glass factories in China. The steel plate used in the renovation of the Verrazano-Narrows Bridge in New York in 2013 came from China, too, not from U.S. Steel, or from any American-based steel plant. Walk through factories in the United States, as I have in recent years, and note the labels on the machines along the assembly lines: more often than not, they are imports from Europe and Asia. The once-ubiquitous American machine tool industry, essential to the manufacture of this equipment, has shrunk considerably.

The upper-echelon executives who supervise many of the nation's factories don't resist these trends, for the simple reason that the multinationals that employ so many of them have factories abroad as well. One of those executives was Colleen Athans, a vice president and general manager at GE, who when I met her in the fall of 2015 supervised a network of factories in the United States and abroad that supplied the parts used in the manufacture of complex jet engines for commercial airliners and for large military aircraft. These giant engines are assembled at two locations: one a recently built factory in Evendale, Indiana, about forty miles east of Cincinnati, and the other an older plant near Paris.[17] I had interviewed Athans's boss, Jeffrey Immelt, GE's chairman and chief executive, several times for this book, and when I asked if I could travel with him for two or three days to GE factories and suppliers—in the United States and/or abroad—he passed me on to Athans, suggesting that I interview her at the Evendale plant, where she had her headquarters, and from which she traveled to a dozen countries to purchase parts and components for the engines.[18]

None of this supply chain is easily visible in Evendale. Nor does the GE assembly line at the plant there behave in a typical, constantly moving fashion. The giant jet engines sit next to one another in one high-ceilinged assembly arena, taking shape as parts and components are brought to each site and fastened into place. This is the propulsion section of the engine, which GE manufactures from the components that Athans's team purchases. "Our supply chain extends over nine countries," she told me, "including the United States, where fifty percent of the components are made."[19]

For one particular model, the propulsion section is GE's contribution to an engine whose front end, the huge rotating fan that propels the aircraft forward, is manufactured by a French company, Safran Aircraft Engines, located in Villaroche, near Paris. Final assembly takes place in both Villaroche and Evendale, with GE shipping some propulsion units to France and Safran sending some of the rotating fans to Evendale. Efficiency gets lost in this ritual exchange, but the two companies, working together, have placed their jointly built engine in a significant number of midsize commercial aircraft, belonging mostly to European airlines.

The largest jet engines manufactured at the Evendale factory are entirely GE's handiwork, and touring the plant, I wondered why GE bothers with the Safran partnership. The answer is straightforward: The companies together sell more engines than either would by itself. Why? Because production across the globe, if aircraft engine factories everywhere all operated flat out, would be greater than what customers across the globe have the wherewithal to purchase. And that is true for many industries. In such a world, multinationals such as GE and Safran find ways to share the available customers, even if that means lowered output for both.

Such companies also rely on the military to supplement civilian consumers. The U.S. military, for example, purchased one out of every four jet engines coming off the line in Evendale in 2015, and while that figure was down from nearly seven out of ten in the late 1980s, it provides vivid evidence that without the subsidies implicit in military purchases, the GE plant might have to close. "Some of those military sales are not just to the Defense Department; they are also to foreign governments," Athans explained.[20] Such payments from foreign governments, like those from Defense, are in effect public subsidies, like the payments that manufacturers receive from U.S. towns and cities. Or as Athans put it, "We certainly expect a certain level of incentive to make a big decision like locating a factory in a city . . . but we kind of stand on our own two feet from there on out. . . . I mean getting better year after year is an absolute necessity."[21] Efficiencies in the manufacturing process at Evendale are certainly a GE achievement; they fall under Athans's motto of getting better year after year. But while GE developed some of the technologies that have made the jet engine a big seller, others originated in research funded by the federal government, which has a right, as a result, to play a role in choosing who gets to purchase an engine, even restricting their sale abroad, although not so much in China.

That nation has become a big consumer of giant jet engines. Anticipating this growth, GE purchased a factory near Shanghai that produces engine components, and these are used in the jet engines manufactured in Evendale. The quid pro quo is straightforward if painful. "Most of the airplanes that are going to be sold in the world over the next decade are going to be sold in China," Athans explained, "and the Chinese have an expectation that if they buy our product, it will help them as well." So GE meets that expectation from its own factory near Shanghai, ignoring the fact that the United States economy would be better off if those components rolled off an assembly line near Evendale (or some other American city). The priority in this case—and in others involving American-based multinationals—is in achieving "competitiveness," even if that means sacrificing factory output in the home country. "I'm not a fan of anything that makes us less competitive," Athans said, reflecting corporate policy.[22] Were that policy different—were it more U.S.-

oriented—total GE production in the United States would rise, and if other multinational manufacturers did the same, the nation's factory output, measured as a share of value added, would rise smartly, perhaps even returning to 1950s levels—or, perhaps more realistically, to 1980s levels.

A national industrial policy, then, would aim in part at increasing production in the United States of the parts and components that go into GE's jet engines, and into numerous other products that are thought of as being made in U.S. factories but are often merely assembled here largely from components manufactured abroad. By some estimates, imported components comprise 20 percent to 30 percent of the total.[23] If that were to diminish, then Athans's role at GE would change, and perhaps diminish, too. So would those of thousands of other executives who carry out similar tasks. Most important, if GE were to make in the United States the jet engine components it imports from its factory near Shanghai, the Chinese would be less likely to purchase GE's jet engines for their aircraft, or so Athans suggests.

The issue, then, is how to break out of this system so that a GE or a GM, along with numerous other multinationals, can manufacture more in the United States and export more from their home country, particularly to China. And the answer is that the multinationals resist going down this perilous road, and probably can't without losing ground to companies that are willing to operate factories in countries where customers are. Reshoring, as a result, has remained a limited activity, designed for products sold principally in America, usually by smaller manufacturers without much of a stake in overseas sales, or by multinationals engaged in developing a new technology.

Athans's responsibilities included a new "additive manufacturing" plant that GE opened in Auburn, Alabama, in 2015. Additive manufacturing is a relatively new technology in which parts (in this case jet engine parts) are manufactured by depositing micro-thin layers of powdery metal one atop another to build up the part, rather than forming it in the traditional way, by using a cutting instrument such as a lathe to machine a part from a solid piece of metal. GE employed the additive technology to make parts for its jet engines at the Auburn factory, which is four hundred miles south of Evendale, placing the factory in Auburn mainly because it outbid other cities. "They have been great partners," Athans said.[24] "Their strategy has been to recruit companies to the area that don't compete with each other, so I'm not competing for the same workforce as the plant down the road from me—so that companies that locate in the area are very complementary to each other. And the city helps us hire people with a whole range of skill sets from university-trained scientists to local trade school graduates to people who come off the streets and can be trained on the job."

That's fine for GE, but Auburn and its people would benefit in the long run from a cluster of factories engaged in additive manufacturing, not just GE's single facility. The competition for workers would drive up wages and encourage the manufacturers to fund apprenticeship programs to train more people. Universities in the area would benefit as the manufacturers funded research into the technology and then shared the results under pressure from a federal industrial policy that funneled subsidies to manufacturers, replacing the regional system of subsidies now built into the intercity competition for a manufacturer's presence. Absent that competition, unions would be more likely to form to represent GE's workers in

Auburn and also the employees of other companies engaged in additive manufacturing, just as they did in the early twentieth century, when auto manufacturers clustered in southern Michigan. Union leaders might even become board members for one or more of the manufacturers, as they now often do in Germany, and their presence as directors would make GE's board, for example, less likely to offshore the production in Auburn.[25]

The administrators of a national industrial policy, seeking greater factory output for the nation, as required by some future Congress in legislation signed by the president, might easily put GE under pressure to cancel the joint production agreement with Safran in favor of making both sections of its engine in the United States, thus contributing to an increase in manufacturing's share of the GDP. Similarly, Boeing, which once manufactured in America all of the wings for its various airliners, would be pressured to do so again, instead of importing some of them from Asia. Indeed, factory owners everywhere in the nation would be required to use in their products a higher percentage of U.S.-made parts and components, cutting back on the roughly one-third that have been imported in the early years of the twenty-first century. Apple would be pressured to assemble its iPhones in the United States rather than in China— and from components made in the United States rather than in Asia. The Eaton Corporation, the assembler of truck transmissions at factories in the Midwest, would be asked to manufacture all of the major components for those transmissions at home. The auto manufacturers would be pressured to shift back to the United States at least some of the assembly now taking place at their factories in northern Mexico. The steel industry would be required to manufacture in the United States *all* of the steel that goes into highways, bridges, schools, and other public infrastructure. The possibilities would seem endless as the administration in office, whatever the party, gradually pushed domestic factory production back north of 19 or 20 percent of GDP—bringing it roughly in line with other major industrial nations.

Factory workers once were labor nobility. Their productivity exceeded that of workers in nearly every other sector, and their pay rose in tandem with their productivity. When ten factory workers, for example, fashioned ten sheets of steel valued at a hundred dollars apiece into ten auto fenders valued at $125 apiece, and did this each hour of their working day, they earned a share of the twenty-five-dollar added value that their labor helped to make possible. Their "productivity" funded their wage, and as the number of fenders produced each hour rose, with the help of ever more efficient machinery and organization, each worker's productivity and wages rose in tandem, as long as unions were present to make this happen. The system functioned until the early 1970s, when the unions' bargaining power started to gradually unravel. From then on, productivity kept rising, as in the past, but wages failed to keep pace. The gains went into profits or into the pay of top managers, while workers' earnings stagnated.

Making matters worse, American multinationals, which accounted for most of the factory production in the United States, located more and more of their new facilities overseas, and relied on exports from those offshore operations to serve global markets. As an economics writer for the *New York Times*, I watched the transition through periodic visits to factories in the 1980s and

1990s, and particularly to The Stanley Works, whose story I told in chapter 4.

Stanley designs and manufactures most of its hand tools, including its famous retractable tape measures, which clip on to workers' belts, all over the world. In most cases, the tools are designed and initially manufactured in a cluster of buildings near the company's headquarters in New Britain, Connecticut. My first contact with The Stanley Works was through its chief executive, Donald W. Davis, whom I had met and gotten to know at meetings of the National Association of Manufacturers, when he was a NAM board member and American manufacturing was still mainly a domestic affair.

Seeking publicity for his company, Davis invited me to visit the New Britain complex, which I did. After he retired in 1987, I continued the relationship with his successor, Richard Ayers, and then with Ayers's successor, John M. Trani. Ayers and Trani were catalysts in the evolution of The Stanley Works into a multinational operation. It was an evolution Davis had initiated and later regretted—as did I, coming reluctantly to the conclusion that short of a well-publicized industrial policy directed from Washington, one that would literally post on LED billboards in Times Square the goal of increasing national manufacturing output to 19 or 20 percent of GDP, reaching that goal just will not happen.

The multinational model is too deeply entrenched. The men and women who run multinationals today are worlds away from the Donald Davis I knew—the Navy officer on active duty in the Pacific during World War II who went to work for The Stanley Works after mustering out and never left, sinking roots into his career and his community. He had been president of New Britain's board of education, among other civic activities, holding that post while several of his six children attended the city's public schools. When the company decided to build a new, larger headquarters in 1985, in a scenic wooded industrial park on the outskirts of New Britain, Davis insisted that the building remain entirely within the city's boundaries, and therefore subject to New Britain's property taxes. He later drove me to the site to show me that the modernistic, three-story structure and its campus were indeed within the city, although one side was just a few feet from the city line. "I think of us as an international company headquartered in New Britain, but I hesitate to use the word *global* because it gives the impression of rootlessness," he told me then.[26]

There had been a few acquisitions—Bostitch in Rhode Island, which makes industrial-quality staplers, stands out—and Davis had opened Stanley Works factories in England, Germany, and Italy. But he put most of his energy and most of the corporate investment into the New Britain complex. He had automated part of the production line for various models of retractable tape measure, including the thirty-five-foot-long Fat Max—a signature product—and he envisioned a fully automated, gradually expanding factory right there in New Britain in the years ahead.

When I met Davis in the mid-1980s, when midsize manufacturing companies such as The Stanley Works were beginning to spread themselves abroad, in the process helping to construct a global system that has limited factory output in the United States, perhaps irreversibly. Davis had not intended to go that far. He had put factories abroad, even in the 1970s, but only to meet the needs of a particular set of overseas customers, such as those in France, who wanted their tape measures manufactured or at least assembled in their own countries, and with measurements in centimeters and meters rather than in inches and feet. In those days, Stanley's sales in the United States were rising briskly just to satisfy domestic demand, so that opening a factory in France or in Italy didn't subtract from U.S. production. Still, the output of those overseas factories substituted for exports from the United States and thus from domestic production that might have been.

When—years later—I said precisely that to Richard Ayers, who succeeded Davis as Stanley's chief executive in 1987, he responded that exporting was not an option during his tenure, and it had ceased to be an option for Davis, too. The French, the British, and the Italians, among others, wanted the coiled steel tape measures manufactured in their towns and cities. A generation after World War II, Europe had been rebuilt, and its nations had asserted themselves. Davis, in response, had accepted their demands, building factories in several European cities. "I don't know if it was the nationalistic feeling in those countries," Ayers recalled, "or consumers who wanted to buy what was made in their countries, or the taxing authorities," but putting factories overseas became unavoidable, although doing so wasn't necessarily as efficient as mass production in and overseas distribution from a single U.S. factory.[27] Given the pressures, a multinational corporate structure emerged— one that could oversee and manage production in numerous countries simultaneously.

After his retirement, Davis and his wife shuttled among homes in Martha's Vineyard and Hobe Sound, Florida, and their Dutch-colonial house in New Britain, which Davis had painted yellow— the same bright shade as the tools his company manufactured. But after a while he and his wife sold their New Britain home, and Davis soon stopped visiting the city altogether. He didn't want to encounter on the streets and in restaurants the numerous Stanley employees who had been laid off as the company evolved into a multinational. "They just moaned about what was happening," he told me. It was too painful, particularly for the man who had initiated the process back in the 1980s. So Davis stayed away, and a year before his death, in 2010, The Stanley Works completed the process he had set in motion, by acquiring Black & Decker, the other big hand-tool manufacturer in the United States. The name was changed to Stanley Black & Decker, and a fully fledged multinational emerged, with semi-autonomous divisions operating factories in Europe and Asia, and revenue from abroad finally exceeding that in the United States.

Long before, in the late 1980s, a federal industrial policy, using subsidies to increase output in the United States, could have altered the trajectory that Davis put in motion, particularly if the policy had required Stanley to preserve its main factory complex in New Britain, where most of the company's signature yellow tools were still manufactured, and even reshore significant amounts of their production in Asia and Europe to bolster output in New Britain. That's a step that multinationals today are very likely to resist. Why should they concentrate production in the United States when free trade agreements such as NAFTA and TPP are designed to give them easy access to the American marketplace from their overseas factories, as well as easy access to European and Asian customers? Stronger unions would help. So would stepped-up subsidies embedded in a national industrial policy that set levels for production within the United States. But the multinationals receive similar subsidies, in one guise or another, from the nations that host their overseas factories.

Too many horses, in sum, are gone from the barn, and unlikely to return.

Afterword

In his bestselling biography *The Wright Brothers*, the journalist and author David McCullough tells the story of the brothers' historic flight, casting it as the achievement of two bicycle mechanics in Dayton, Ohio, whose ingenuity and focused determination ushered in the age of propeller-driven aircraft. The Wright brothers belong in the front ranks of this particularly American pantheon. But to get their craft into the air on December 17, 1903, Orville and Wilbur needed the factories that were then industrializing the Midwest. Above all, they had to limit their craft's weight, which they did by installing a gasoline engine lighter than the cast-iron motors then being used in the autos of the day. At their request, the Aluminum Company of America (Alcoa) had cast the engine block and crankcase in this new, lighter metal at Alcoa's expanding factory in Pittsburgh, which had opened just fifteen years before the Wrights placed their order. The aluminum in their motor was not yet fully patented, but without it, the plane that flew at Kitty Hawk would not have gotten off the ground.[1]

The plane's very existence depended not only on aluminum but also on the numerous components that the brothers were able to purchase "from Dayton manufacturers and suppliers," as Mc-Cullough notes. Engine-driven flight was not their achievement alone: it was also the collective achievement of a rapidly growing manufacturing sector that Wilbur and Orville could cherry-pick for the materials and subassemblies they needed.[2]

Over the next eighty years, that combination of inventiveness and factory production, spreading out from the Northeast and Midwest, made the United States the world leader in manufacturing, and the hourly workers in the factories gradually fought for their share. In the 1960s and 1970s, when union membership and bargaining power were at their peak, roughly 75 percent of a factory's revenue flowed to labor. As a result, tens of thousands of blue-collar factory workers earned enough to purchase the trappings of middle-class life, and widely circulated magazines such as *Life* ran spreads making this point.

By 2016, however, labor's share had fallen to less than 55 percent, and the spotlight had shifted from upward to downward mobility. In hindsight, the reasons were clear enough. The largest manufacturers had morphed into multinational operations, and they used their global factory networks to make in other countries more and more of what they sold in those countries—and in the United States, too.[3] A significant share of the nation's hourly workers had been employed by multinationals in their American factories, and as those multinationals shifted production abroad, employment in American factories deteriorated, along with union membership and wage levels. That happened even for assembly line workers at auto factories represented by the powerful United Auto Workers, which finally gave ground—accepting a lower wage scale for those hired after

2007. And there the matter stood until the fall of 2015, when UAW negotiators, under pressure from younger members whose earnings were stuck on the lower tier, finally negotiated contract language phasing out that lower tier.

Karl Hoeltge, a twenty-two-year-old who had completed two years of community college, was one. He was earning fifteen dollars an hour on the assembly line at a General Motors factory near St. Louis when I first interviewed him, in 2012. He earned that wage under a UAW contract that capped his "lower-tier" pay on the factory's assembly line at a lifetime maximum of $19.28 an hour. In contrast, Karl's father, Gary Hoeltge, working on the same assembly line— sometimes within sight of his son—earned twenty-nine dollars an hour, the top wage for hourly workers hired before the introduction in 2007 of the lower tier in the UAW contract. Understandably, Karl was upset. Although better educated than his father, he was not doing as well. "I won't leave GM until I have something better, and I look all the time for something better," he told me.[4] Months later, he was still at GM, still looking for something better.

Jobs on factory assembly lines were and continue to be the best avenue to middle-class incomes for men and women with only a high school education. The assembly of finished products from numerous components does not require a lot of formal education, but it nevertheless generates more value added than most other lines of work. The wage share of that value added is fatter when the workers receiving it are organized into unions and can thus bargain more effectively for a significant portion. Workers' leverage dissipated, however, as production moved offshore. Rather than flowing into factory expansion in the United States, investment now flowed disproportionately into putting factories abroad, to serve not just the

American market but rising consumption in other countries. In 1989, for example, when Cyril Siewert, then the CFO of the Colgate-Palmolive Company, declared, "There is no mindset that puts this country [the United States] first," his statement made front-page news.[5] A top executive of an iconic American company had openly, even shamelessly, embraced globalization; in fact Colgate-Palmolive was already manufacturing more toothpaste, soaps, and toiletries outside the United States than inside. But people gasped at Siewert's admission. Twenty-five years later, such statements were too obvious to even be quoted, much less on the front page.

Given the power of the multinationals, and the weakness of unions, there is only one viable route to restoring manufacturing in America and with it the standard of living that had become so essential to millions of working Americans. The White House and Congress must step in with legislation that bluntly requires manufacturers, particularly the multinationals, to increase the value of what they make in the United States back up to at least 17 or 18 percent of GDP, from 12 percent in 2016.

There are sensible arguments for increasing the government's role in crafting an industrial policy along these lines, not the least of them being that government already contributes overwhelmingly to innovation and productivity in the private sector. That first Apple desktop computer evolved from federally funded research, not from the head of Steve Jobs. He played a role, of course, as inventor and marketer, but he stood on the shoulders of publicly employed scientists working in government laboratories conducting research in basic science that made the first Apple desktop computer possible. The same is true for the big jet engines mounted in the tens of thousands on commercial aircraft, likewise the touch-screen technology integrated into iPads and iPhones, and the initial research for numerous miracle drugs that pharmaceutical companies eventually manufacture.

The list is voluminous, as Mariana Mazzucato, a British economist, explained in *The Entrepreneurial State: Debunking Public vs. Private Sector Myths*, a book that sold briskly when it was published in 2013, calling attention to government's huge role in inventing what factories make.[6] Contrary to received ideas, Mazzucato shows, the federal government took the risks and bore the costs of the breakthroughs in computer technology that allowed Jobs and his colleagues to develop that first desktop computer in his garage, if you wish. Similarly, the navigational devices now installed in most cars assembled in the United States are directly dependent upon the global positioning system (GPS)—developed by the Department of Defense in the 1970s to accurately pinpoint enemy positions and targets. Public spending, it turns out, is the font of innovation. Or as Mazzucato's book makes clear: "The history of new sectors teaches us that private investments tend to wait for the early high-risk investments to be made first by the State."[7]

The question, then, is not whether to have a federal industrial policy but whether to recognize the industrial policies that already exist at the federal, state, and municipal levels. Having recognized these, we must press our elected officials to organize them efficiently and fairly, with the goal of increasing factory output as a share of the American economy to a level that, at the very least, restores the nation's trade surplus and puts factory employment once again on an upward trajectory. The best bet for more production as a share of the total economy would be to replace with federal subsidies those that nearly every manufacturer now receives from state and municipal governments as lures to locate in one community rather than another. Such a new system of federal subsidies would have a clear national goal: make in the United States much more of the merchandise that multinationals now manufacture abroad. The multinationals would almost certainly resist a national policy that not only routed subsidies through Washington but in doing so pressured them to bring home a sizeable share of their overseas production, by setting rules for the minimum percentage of total output that must be located in the United States. In this regard, free trade agreements have been wonderful for multinationals, but they have encouraged the GMs and GEs to disregard nationality as they pursue production arrangements that are optimal for them if not for the United States. Under a nationally oriented industrial policy, these agreements would be canceled or allowed to expire, thus increasing the risks for multinationals serving the American market from factories abroad. Given the support that free trade has gotten over the years from both major political parties, the cancellation of existing trade agreements does not seem likely, although for the millions of hourly workers who would normally staff our domestic factories, there are few if any alternatives that would restore to them an adequate standard of living.

A national industrial policy designed to raise factory output in the United States is, at this advanced stage in the globalization of manufacturing, quite a stretch. Pulling it off might even require a moratorium on corporate mergers in which, in the name of achieving efficiencies, factories have been closed, shrinking domestic output. We would have to acknowledge, moreover, that duplication and overproduction are potentially more humane than efficiency. They increase blue-collar factory employment and they also shrink the trade deficit as imports are replaced with more costly merchandise made in the United States. These seem to me reasonable returns for the numerous subsidies that the manufacturing process requires.

Less free trade would prompt more factory production within the United States or, alternatively, would pressure Americans to give up some of the consumption-oriented lifestyle that free trade has helped to make possible by opening the nation's borders to an endless flood of relatively inexpensive merchandise manufactured in other countries. Without this flow, the consequences would soon kick in: Instead of two cars per family, for example, we would go back to one, plus a motor-scooter perhaps, neither of them gas guzzlers. We would also be under pressure to make greater use of public transportation, a trend that, in time, might revive cities as places in which to live and put factories, and address the civil rights issue described in chapter 3.

Free trade seems likely to endure until it provokes a crisis of its own. Eventually, the annual trade deficits that free trade encourages will erode the value of the U.S. dollar vis-à-vis other currencies. Gradually, the Chinese and the Europeans will become reluctant to accept dollars in exchange for what they sell us. To convince them to keep selling to us we will have to pay more and more in dollars for what we purchase. As imports become expensive in dollar terms, the dollar itself will lose its standing as the world's bedrock currency, the one that determines the value or purchasing power of other currencies. The euro or the Chinese renminbi will take on that role, just as the U.S. dollar did in the twentieth century, when it replaced the British pound. The reason: American factory output overwhelmed that of the British, and of the other industrial nations, as their factories were destroyed during World War II. Since the war, however, and particularly since the 1950s, factory construction and output have risen more rapidly abroad than in the United States. The question then becomes how to reverse this trend, or at least to moderate it. Higher factory output within the United States, the chief goal of a new industrial policy, would also mean more factory jobs, and more security for existing jobs. With luck, the overall number would move back toward, even if it would never reach, the peaks of 16.6 million people in 1943 and 19.5 million in 1979. In 1979, factory employment represented 22 percent of all civilian employment—far above the 8 percent as 2016 came to a close. A federal industrial policy would have as a goal an increase in this percentage. It would also require manufacturers to stand aside as their employees vote on whether to be represented by unions. It would require such votes at every factory site—the goal being to resurrect President Franklin Delano Roosevelt's historic (and now almost forgotten) attempt to implement a second bill of rights, in the mid-1940s, when employment in manufacturing played a much bigger role than in 2016. In this second bill of rights—proposed in FDR's State of the Union address on January 11, 1944—the constitution would guarantee employment at decent wages to every adult citizen who wanted a job. Manufacturers would have to play a big part in fulfilling that promise. In 1944, they employed 38 percent of the civilian workforce, and would continue to employ above 30 percent for more than a decade.[8] Not surprisingly, union membership—a parallel component of the Roosevelt proposal— followed a similar trajectory. And then, as manufacturing's presence in the economy shrank, so did union power, undermining the most important clause in Roosevelt's second bill of rights: "The right to a useful and remunerative job in the industries or shops or farms or mines of the nation."

Two generations later, can we resurrect Roosevelt's second bill of rights as a pressing political issue? That seems doubtful, unless we can accept that manufacturing is, by its nature, a market activity sustained by public subsidies, and those subsidies entail an obligation—namely to respond to the needs of millions of people whose taxes fund the subsidies.

Above all, a national industrial policy that dispersed billions of dollars in subsidies would be rooted in precedent. Out of the Dust Bowl and the Great Depression in the 1930s, and the worldwide demand for American farm produce during and after World War II, came billions of dollars in federal subsidies to sustain farming and protect farmers' incomes from poor harvests. The political maneuvering involved in authorizing the annual farm subsidy once drew headlines and controversy, but now rarely does. We accept that farming is a federally subsidized market activity. Manufacturing must proceed along a similar path.

My fear is that this necessity won't become apparent to most Americans; that we will acquiesce to manufacturing's shrunken role in the American economy, just as we gradually acquiesced to frequent large-scale layoffs in the late twentieth century—a process I described in my first book, *The Disposable American: Layoffs and Their Consequences* (2006). This second book, I have finally realized, is a sequel to the first. Just as we acquiesced to layoffs, we have acquiesced to the numerous factory closings that produced, and still produce, so many of the layoffs. The damage to individual

American workers' self-esteem from layoffs, no matter what the reason for them, is enduring. And so is the damage to upward mobility, to decent urban life, to civil rights, to the value of the dollar, and, ultimately, to everyone's standard of living that manufacturing makes possible.

Notes

1. The Long Unwinding

1. One television program that attempts to counter this indifference to manufacturing and foster wonderment is *How It's Made* (*Comment C'est Fait* in French), a series of half-hour television documentaries produced in the Canadian province of Quebec by Productions MAJ/Productions MAJ 2 and broadcast on the Science channel in the United States. Each episode takes viewers step by step through the production processes used to make several everyday products, following the ingenious assembly lines that yield tires, stoves, wineglasses, tableware, bottled orange juice, batteries, chainsaws, handbags, bubble gum, engines, guitars, and snowboards, among numerous other items.

2. See Marc Levinson, "U.S. Manufacturing in International Perspective," Congressional Research Service, Apr. 26, 2016. (Levinson is a section research manager at the CRS.) In 2014, the most recent year for which statistics were available, the sector accounted for $2.928 trillion worth of annual GDP for China, versus $2.098 trillion for the United States. China's manufacturing output, measured in dollars as valued added, has risen sharply since 2004, and first surpassed that of the United States in 2010.

3. By another measure, computers and electronics dominate the growth of factory output in the United States: when these sectors are separated out from the aggregate statistics, the remaining manufacturing industries show a decline in output, according to Robert D. Atkinson, president of the Information and

Technology Innovation Foundation in Washington (interview with the author, Aug. 3, 2012). Atkinson makes the same point in his book *Innovation Economics: the Race for Global Advantage* (New Haven: Yale University Press, 2012), co-authored with Stephen J. Ezell, a senior analyst at the foundation. So does Susan N. Houseman, a senior economist at the W.E. Upjohn Institute in Kalamazoo, Michigan, and a pioneer in this research.

4. U.S. multinationals—that is, multinationals headquartered in the United States—accounted for 66.5 percent of manufacturing value added within the country in 2010, according to the Commerce Department's Bureau of Economic Analysis. That percentage has held steady for more than twenty-five years and continues to do so in the current decade. Value added in manufacturing is the sector's standard measure of output. When, for example, a sheet of steel valued at one hundred dollars is stamped into a fender valued at $125, the value added is twenty-five dollars. See Kevin B. Barefoot, "U.S. Multinational Companies: Operations of U.S. Parents and Their Foreign Affiliates in 2010," *Survey of Current Business*, November 2012, www.bea.gov/scb/pdf/2012/11%20November/1112MNCs.pdf. By this measure, the U.S. economy generated $18 trillion in value added in 2015, with manufacturers contributing $2 trillion, or 11 percent, of this amount, and multinational manufacturers nearly two-thirds of the $2 trillion total, or $1.2 trillion. See also the work of Susan Houseman, senior economist at the W.E. Upjohn Institute, in Kalamazoo, Michigan, who wrote in an October 2016 paper, reiterating an earlier finding: "Manufacturing's anemic output growth is largely the result of globalization, and that fact (coupled with automation) is responsible for the large reductions in manufacturing employment since the 1990's."

5. Garment manufacturing survived in New York into the twenty-first century, centered in the Garment District around 38th Street between Seventh and Eighth Avenues. See Rebecca Mead, "The Garmento King: Can Andrew Rosen, of Theory, Keep Manhattan Humming with Sewing Machines?," *New Yorker*, Sep. 23, 2013.

6. In the jargon of economic theory, this was the supply-side solution that many politicians, business executives, and academics championed in the 1980s and still do, preferring this way of thinking to one that emphasizes demand. Supply creates its own demand, to quote the father of supply-side economics, Jean-Baptiste Say (1767–1832), a French economist whose life overlapped

Adam Smith's. Equip workers with skills, Say argued, and jobs will material-ize that require those skills. Taking the theory a step further, customers will likewise materialize to purchase the merchandise (or the services) that the skilled workers produce. Some of those customers would be the newly skilled workers themselves. They would use their incomes from their new jobs to pur-chase goods and services.

Supply thus creates its own demand. Ronald Reagan offered this view as a justification for cutting taxes. If taxes were lowered, he argued, the beneficia-ries of those lowered taxes, particularly the wealthy, would invest the money saved in new productive activity, confident that customers would materialize from among the newly skilled workers employed in the new productive facili-ties. The beneficiaries of the Reagan tax cuts, however, hesitated. They weren't so sure that newly skilled workers would spend the money they earned. In-stead, they might save their money, in case they lost their jobs before they had put aside enough to weather a stretch of unemployment. Years before, John Maynard Keynes had recognized this shortcoming in supply-side theory. His solution, set forth in *The General Theory of Employment, Interest and Money*, published in 1936, argued that government should increase its spending during recessions, in effect replacing insufficient spending in the general population. President Franklin Delano Roosevelt did exactly that through his New Deal policies, and the Reagan administration ended up doing it as well, partly through stepped-up spending on weapons manufacturing. Yet the supply-side argument didn't die. During his 2016 campaign for president, Donald Trump proposed a tax cut on high-end incomes as a means of stimulating investment. In doing so, he ignored that demand for products and services drives investment in the fa-cilities needed to produce or sell the sought-after products and services.

7. According to Edward Alden and Rebecca Strauss, a senior fellow and an associate director, respectively, at the Council on Foreign Relations, each year state and local governments spend more than $80 billion, or roughly 7 percent of their total budgets, on tax breaks and outright cash subsidies to companies in every industry to induce them to locate, or relocate, in their cities and states. The State of Washington, for example, granted to Boeing in 2013 a subsidy package valued at $8.7 billion to prevent the company from moving produc-tion to South Carolina, the largest such package of incentives ever granted to a single company in the United States.

8. The information in this paragraph is distilled from reporting trips made over several years to Rome, New York; Midland, Michigan; and Louisville, Kentucky.

9. The figures are from the World Bank and the Commerce Department's Bureau of Economic Analysis.

10. Ibid.

11. See the chart at data.bls.gov/pdq/SurveyOutputServlet on the Department of Labor's Bureau of Labor statistics website.

12. Ibid.

13. Ibid.

14. See two sets of data: manufacturing employment, at data.bls.gov/pdq /SurveyOutputServlet, and the labor force participation rate, at the same website. The labor force participation rate is the percentage of the population sixteen years or older either employed or officially unemployed, which means without a job but "actively seeking" one. Those who have lost a job but are not actively seeking another are not counted as unemployed and are therefore not considered to be in the labor force. These tables are based on monthly surveys of 65,000 households, representing a cross-section of the nation's population. From these surveys come the unemployment rate, which has also edged up over the years. See data.bls.gov/pdq/SurveyOutputServlet.

15. See Jeff Madrick, *The Case for Big Government* (Princeton, NJ: Princeton University Press, 2009), 40.

16. See for example U.S. Department of Commerce, Bureau of Economic Analysis, www.bea.gov/newsreleases/industry/gdpindustry/2016/pdf/gdpind116 .pdf, Table 8.

17. Racism also played a role in the Argentine assertion of European identity. The country's population is overwhelmingly white, to this day. The slave trade brought Africans in huge numbers to neighboring Brazil to cultivate and harvest sugar and other labor-intensive crops. The Argentine beef industry, by contrast, required relatively little labor. Cattle grazed untended on the pampa grasslands that encircled Buenos Aires and radiated westward for hundreds of miles. In the temperate climate, snow rarely fell and the temperature almost never dropped below freezing, so cattle grew up almost on their own. The relatively few gauchos employed to round up the mature animals and herd them to slaughterhouses or to railroads were impoverished white

men, descended from Europeans. The indigenous peoples who had inhabited Argentina in precolonial times were drastically reduced in numbers from the seventeenth through the nineteenth centuries by European diseases, colonial wars, enslavement, and mestization. Moreover, former African slaves in neighboring Brazil did not as freed people migrate to Argentina; by staying away, they avoided the racism among white Argentines well into the twentieth century, and also the risk of being slaughtered as many of Argentina's indigenous peoples had been. In my day, 99 percent of the population, or even more, identified as descendants of white Europeans. (However, genetic studies in the twenty-first century have shown that about one-third of the population—and in some Argentine provinces, more than twice that level—have Amerindian heritage. See en.wikipedia.org/wiki/Indigenous_peoples _in_Argentina.)

18. Cognitive psychologists such as Eldar Shafir of Princeton University recognize this phenomenon. "We carry within us these different identities," Shafir explained in a telephone interview. These identities assert themselves more forcefully when we are away from our country. Or as Shafir put it, "We all know that we feel more American in London than in New York."

19. Susan N. Houseman, at the W.E. Upjohn Institute in Kalamazoo, Michigan, among others.

20. See Louis Uchitelle, "Surge in Jobs Mostly Bypasses the Factory Floor," *New York Times*, May 11, 2004; and "Made in the U.S.A. (Except for the Parts)," *New York Times*, Apr. 8, 2005.

21. Wilson's remark is commonly misquoted as "What's good for General Motors is good for the country." The misquotation is in itself telling. See Justin Hyde, "GM's 'Engine Charlie' Wilson Learned to Live with a Misquote," *Detroit Free Press*, Sept. 14, 2008.

22. See Louis Uchitelle, "Is Manufacturing Falling Off the Radar?" *New York Times*, Sep. 10, 2011.

23. The committee members were Steven Rattner, a Wall Street executive, Ron Bloom, a USW official who later joined the Wall Street firm Lazard Frères and Company (today Lazard), and Gene Sperling, director of the National Economic Council in the Obama administration from 2009 until 2013.

24. The statistic is derived from U.S. Census Bureau data. Only factories that once had employed at least twenty people were included in the

calculation. I am indebted to research assistant Aaron Freedman for compiling the U.S. Census data.

25. See industrial production and capacity utilization at www.federalreserve .gov/releases/g17/current.

2. Redefining Skill

1. See Mark Twain, *Life on the Mississippi* (Cambridge, Mass.: H.O. Houghton and Company, 1874, 1875).

2. Richard Sennett is a professor emeritus at New York University. This quote is from a telephone interview on June 12, 2013.

3. Kobacker Stores was headquartered then in Columbus, Ohio. The Kobacker family sold the chain in 1996 to Payless Shoes in a deal valued at the time at $40 to $50 million.

4. Many mid-twentieth century CEOs died in the 1980s and 1990s, and their obituaries described these early beginnings.

5. President Franklin D. Roosevelt signed the G.I. Bill into law on June 22, 1944. In its peak year, 1947, veterans accounted for 47 percent of all college admissions, according to the Department of Veterans Affairs. The original G.I. Bill expired on July 25, 1956. In 2008, the G.I. Bill was updated. "The new law," according to the Bureau of Veterans Affairs, "gives Veterans with active duty service on, or after, Sept. 11 2001, enhanced educational benefits that cover more educational expenses, provide a living allowance, money for books and the ability to transfer unused educational benefits to spouses or children." See www.benefits.va.gov/gibill/history.asp.

6. When mass corporate layoffs began to occur with some frequency in the 1980s, numerous media accounts described what was, in effect, the end of de facto job security in the post–World War II years. As the layoffs continued and increasingly involved college-educated workers, the public acquiesced and media accounts became less frequent.

7. See Harry Braverman, *Labor and Monopoly Capitalism: The Degradation of Work in the Twentieth Century* (New York: Monthly Review Press, 1974), 148–51.

8. Ibid.

9. See Louis Uchitelle, "Detroit's Woes Wound an Army of Suppliers," *New York Times*, June 2, 2009.

10. Ruth Milkman, *Farewell to the Factory: Auto Workers in the Late Twentieth Century* (Berkeley: University of California Press, 1997); and Louis Uchitelle's Business Day essay, "A Nation That's Losing Its Toolbox," *New York Times*, July 21, 2012.

11. For background on ATS, see its website: www.advancedtech.com /about-us.

12. Telephone interview with Donald K. Johnson, Nov. 11, 2014.

13. Interview with Donald K. Johnson, Nov. 6, 2014, at a factory in Chicago.

14. Ibid.

15. Telephone interview with Jeffrey Owens, Feb. 1, 2011.

16. The interview took place at the chocolate factory on Nov. 7, 2014.

17. Ibid.

18. According to the company, the wages paid to ATS technicians skilled in maintaining machinery ranged from $50,000 to $80,000 a year in 2014.

19. See www.bls.gov/news.release/pdf/union2.pdf. See also www.bls.gov /news.release/history/union2_01182001.txt.

20. Telephone interview, Nov. 25, 2013. Issa later became vice president and general manager of Regal Beloit Corporation, which had acquired Milwaukee Gear in 2012.

21. Quoted by Dave Jamieson and Arthur Delaney, "Obama State of the Union Speech Calls for Job Training, Unemployment Insurance Reform," *Huffington Post*, Jan. 2, 2012.

22. In his 2017 budget proposal, President Obama called for a $2 billion Apprenticeship Training Fund to greatly increase the number of apprentices in the nation. He had pushed for similar spending earlier in his presidency to help high-school graduates who didn't want to go on to college.

23. This is the so-called U6 rate of unemployment, the broadest measure of unemployment used by the Bureau of Labor Statistics. U6 includes the officially unemployed, part-timers seeking more hours of work, and people who say they want a job but are too discouraged to continue looking for one.

24. Leaders of the nation's multinational corporations saw in this reasoning an opportunity to open offices and factories overseas while minimizing the opposition back home to such expansion. The Chamber of Commerce and

NAM also endorsed the strategy, although not without opposition from some smaller manufacturers within NAM who had factories only in the United States. Some of these smaller manufacturers supplied parts and components to larger ones, and as these larger companies opened factories abroad, the smaller operations gradually followed suit. See, for example, Louis Uchitelle, "Globalization: It's Not Just Wages: For Whirlpool, High-Cost Germany Can Still Have Advantages," *New York Times*, June 17, 2005.

25. I don't want to oversimplify this point. Plainly a chemist, a lawyer, a physicist, an engineer, or an elementary school teacher is a skilled person, and acquiring their skills means earning at least a bachelor's degree. In the nineteenth and early twentieth centuries, however, even such skills were often commonly acquired through apprenticeships or on-the-job training, without college. On-the-job training or experience still elevates a college-trained rookie in teaching or medicine to the level of a skilled teacher and doctor.

26. Procter & Gamble made most of its soap products in the greater Cincinnati area until the late twentieth century, and GE Aviation in 2016 still manufactured jet aircraft engines there, in a fifty-fifty partnership with Safran Aircraft Engines (formerly Snecma), a unit of the French aerospace giant Safran. The front-end rotary section of each engine was made in a factory near Paris and the rest of the engine in a factory on the outskirts of Cincinnati, and the two units were shipped to one plant or the other for final assembly. The forty-year-old partnership operated under the name CFM International.

27. See Louis Uchitelle, "Long Before Recent Unrest, Cincinnati Simmered," *New York Times*, May 1, 2001.

28. Interview in Mullett's office at Eagle Tech in Columbia City, Indiana, Nov. 29, 2012.

29. See the Bureau of Labor Statistics chart at data.bls.gov/pdq/Survey OutputServlet.

3. Urban Manufacturing

1. Ford closed the plant in 2006, laying off 1,445 workers. See "Ford Closes Hazelwood Plant, Lays Off 1,445 Workers," *St. Louis Business Journal*, Jan. 23, 2006, www.bizjournals.com/stlouis/stories/2006/01/23/daily1.html. The St. Louis Brewery Apartments opened in 1985, according to Wikipedia, and include three buildings acquired from Falstaff Brewery.

2. The original name, bestowed in 1860, was the Charles Wunderlich Cooperage Company. As the technology changed, the company divided into two operations, Wunderlich Barrel Manufacturing and Wunderlich Fibre Box Company. The latter eventually became the company's only name.

3. Interviews with Robert Wunderlich and visits to his factory on Aug. 5, 2013, and Mar. 30, 2014. A third interview took place on Oct. 1, 2014, during a visit to St. Louis but not to the factory. On a fourth visit, in Sept. 2016, Robert Wunderlich's son, Robert A. Wunderlich Jr., joined us and did most of the talking. By then he was well on is his way to succeeding his father as the sixth generation Wunderlich to run the company, teamed with a brother-in-law, Steven Dybus.

4. The Wunderlichs purchased enough land on which to build a factory with eight thousand square feet of space, which actually was less than they would have bought, Robert Wunderlich said, if more land had been available in the neighborhood.

5. "We're not pushing to have that note forgiven because we don't want to pay a capital gains tax on the $200,000," Wunderlich told me in 2014.

6. Assembly of the third vehicle, the Corvette sports car, moved to a GM plant in Bowling Green, Kentucky.

7. Interview with Van Simpson, president of UAW Local 2250, on Sept. 18, 2014, at the local's headquarters in Wentzville, next door to the GM plant.

8. Nearly 40 percent of the 2,200 workers at the Wentzville factory are black. The population of Wentzville has increased from four thousand before GM built the plant in 1983 to 29,070 in 2016, according to the Census Bureau. The total included 26,122, or 89 percent, who were white, and 1,738, or 5 percent, who were African American. See suburbanstats.org/population /missouri/how-many-people-live-in-wentzville.

9. Interview with Simpson, Sept. 18, 2014 (see note 7, above).

10. Interview with Wagman at a coffee shop near his home in St. Louis, Apr. 2, 2014.

11. Interview on Sept. 6, 2016, in St. Louis with Darin Gilley, a former president of UAW Local 1760, representing 4,300 hourly workers at the GM plant in Wentzville. One thousand of the 4,300 are classified as temps and 3,300 as regular hourly workers, Gilley explained. He was among the temps, having been hired for the assembly line at the Wentzville plant in 2007. Under the UAW contract then in effect, his pay topped out at $22 an hour.

12. Measured in jobs, urban manufacturing, defined as factories located in "central counties," lost jobs from 1980 to 2010, while "outlying counties" gained them, according to *The 2014 State New Economy Index*, published by the Information Technology and Innovation Foundation. From 2000 through 2010, both lost jobs, but the urban decline was greater. See www2.itif.org/2014-state-new-economy-index.pdf.

13. They are Barnes-Jewish Hospital, associated with Washington University, and Saint Louis University Hospital, associated with St. Louis University School of Medicine.

14. Telephone interview in May 2014 with Sukalo, who was then working from the company's New York office at 360 West 31st Street.

15. By August 2013, when I first interviewed McKee, he had accumulated 270 of those acres, using tax increment financing, or TIF, to purchase the land. A TIF loan postpones repayment. It is based on the assumption that current improvements, in this case real estate development, will result in future increases in tax revenue, and that these gains will help to justify the initial development loans.

16. Interview with Paul McKee and his wife, Midge, Aug. 13, 2013, at their busy, jerry-built offices in the midst of the scrubland they had purchased. He told me he had acquired the right to purchase up to 1,500 acres in the city, a portion of it once-private land that the city had acquired because of nonpayment of taxes.

17. Ibid.

18. See Nicholas J.C. Pistor, "Aldermen Approve $20 Million Loan to Buy Land for National Geospatial-Intelligence Agency," *St. Louis Post-Dispatch*, July 10, 2015, www.stltoday.com/news/local/govt-and-politics/aldermen-approve-million-loan-to-buy-land-for-national-geospatial/article_42829d7c-4b13-50a2-ab23-a0285bbabb41.html.

19. Interview in St. Louis, Aug. 5, 2013.

20. In addition, in the case of St. Louis, an agreement signed in 1872 formally separated the city from the surrounding St. Louis County and limited land available within the city for new factories. That limit helps to explain the former prevalence of multistory factory construction, and the subsequent practice of putting modern single-story factories outside the city, where more land was available. "When we went from multistory to single-story factories,

that forced manufacturers out of the city; they didn't have the acres they needed to expand within the city," Ruth Keenoy, preservation specialist at the Landmarks Association of St. Louis, told me in an interview on Mar. 31, 2014.

21. These examples are drawn from E.D. Kargau, *Mercantile Industrial and Professional St. Louis* (St. Louis: Nixon-Jones Printing, 1902). The 674-page text is available at archive.org/stream/mercantileindust00karg#page/n7/mode /2up.

22. The pioneering companies that made cars in St. Louis in those days included the Dorris Motor Car Company and Moon Motors. According to Wikipedia, George Preston Dorris developed and patented the gasoline engine float carburetor. Joseph W. Moon, a carriage maker, founded the eponymous Moon Motor Car Company, which made trucks as well as cars, reaching peak production of 10,271 vehicles in 1925.

23. Company ownership has changed hands several times since 1978. The current owner is GlaxoSmithKline.

24. Telephone interviews, May 6, 2014, and Sept. 8, 2016.

25. The day I visited, the lines I saw were delivering more than 3,100 bottles and 1,950 cans a minute. Each contained twelve ounces of beer.

26. See www.anheuser-busch.com/index.php/our-heritage/history/national -landmarks. In 2008, Anheuser-Busch, founded in 1852, was acquired by a European company, InBev. Under the terms of the merger agreement, according to Wikipedia, all of the shares of Anheuser-Busch were acquired for $70 apiece, or a total of $52 billion. The brewery itself was founded in 1852 by Adolphus Busch, a German immigrant, and his father-in-law, Eberhard Anheuser.

27. Anheuser-Busch owns and operates twelve breweries in the United States, eight of them in smaller cities than St. Louis. See anheuser-busch.com /index.php/our-company/operations/breweries-brewery-tours.

28. The concept of value added is defined in chapter 1, note 4. When strong unions are in place as bargaining agents for workers, then workers' share of value added paid in wages is almost always greater than when unions aren't present. Moreover, no industry generates more value added per hour worked than manufacturing, according to the Department of Commerce Bureau of Economic Analysis. So, in theory, hourly wages in manufacturing can be high relative to occupations in other industries.

29. Interview in St. Louis, Apr. 1, 2014, during a second visit to the factory. A son-in-law, Steven Dybus, older than Robert Jr., was also a Wunderlich executive at the time—in fact president of the company while Robert Jr. was in the Marine Corps; a post he continued to hold after Robert Jr.'s return. "If it wasn't for him," Robert Jr. told me, referring to his brother-in-law, "there would not have been that much of a company to come back to after my time in the service." We were speaking by phone in late October, 2016.

30. The interviews with Dr. Suggs took place by telephone on May 4, 2014, and on visits to his newspaper's offices on Oct. 1, 2014, and Sept. 6, 2016.

31. The visit took place on Aug. 5, 2013.

32. Passenger trains moved from Eads Bridge through one tunnel and freight trains through another, the latter surfacing in time to pull into Cupples Station, which was in a different location from the passenger station and handled only freight.

33. Interview in St. Louis, Aug. 8, 2013.

34. Interview and visit to the Brentwood operation, Aug. 9, 2013. Epstein died on Sept. 10, 2014, at the age of seventy-nine.

35. Ibid.

36. Ibid.

37. The National Labor Relations Act of 1935, also known as the Wagner Act after New York senator Robert F. Wagner, is a foundational statute of U.S. labor law, guaranteeing the basic rights of private-sector employees to organize into trade unions, engage in collective bargaining, strike, and so on.

38. See ASPEQ Holding Inc., "About Us," www.aspeqholdings.com/about -us.html. As of May 30, 2014, ASPEQ Heating Group held majority ownership in three companies, each of them a manufacturer of commercial heating devices. Two of these, INDEECO and AccuTherm, were in Missouri and one, Heatrex, was in Meadville, Pennsylvania, notwithstanding ASPEQ's stated goal of confining its holdings to the St. Louis area. Meadville and St. Louis are more than 640 miles apart. In June 2015, Bunker Hill Capital, a private equity firm headquartered in Boston, acquired ASPEQ Heating Group. Bunker Hill's announcement of the acquisition stated that the "majority-holder of ASPEQ, John Eulich, and ASPEQ's senior management team both reinvested meaningful proceeds in the deal." See www.aspeqheating.com/in-the-news .html.

39. William Julius Wilson, *When Work Disappears: The World of the New Urban Poor* (New York: Knopf, 1996), 29–30.

40. Ibid

41. Charles Murray, *Losing Ground: American Social Policy, 1950–1980* (New York: Basic Books, 1984).

42. As quoted by Paul Krugman in his opinion column in the *New York Times*, Mar. 17, 2014. Ryan was then chairman of the House Committee on the Budget. He was elected speaker of the House in October 2015.

43. The name of the business was Moss & Lowenhaupt. These were family names. After attending the University of Michigan but not graduating (his father did not see the need for a diploma and called him home after three years), my grandfather joined a small retail business that relatives had started in St. Louis and built it into a complex commercial operation without changing the name.

44. Tobacco leaves were imported from Cuba, and also some finished cigars, until Fidel Castro's rise to power in 1959. The subsequent embargo of Cuban goods cut off that supply.

45. I learned these details from an interview on Sept. 26, 2014, with Rosalind Williams, a retired city planning director in Ferguson, and during a visit to Ferguson on Sept. 29, 2014. See also Peter Downs, "Ferguson: A String of Betrayals," *Labor Notes*, Aug. 20, 2014, labornotes.org/blogs/2014/08/ferguson-string-betrayals.

46. Scullin Steel started out manufacturing steel railroad ties. It switched to bomb casings during World War II, and survived into the 1960s.

47. Monsanto conducts much of its U.S. research and development at its Chesterfield Village Research Center, in a suburb of St. Louis.

4. Subsidies

1. From the text of Vice President Biden's speech at NAM's spring meeting in Washington, June 10, 2014. Text provided by the Office of the Vice President in an e-mail to me on June 23, 2014, from Stephen Spector, Biden's assistant press secretary.

2. More than 220 congressional meetings were scheduled during the 2014 Summit, NAM reported. See www.nam.org/Events/Manufacturing-Summit/2014/Summit-Highlights.

3. The value of total factory output in the United States, including weapons, measured as value added, was nearly $4 trillion at an annual rate at the end of 2015, according to the Commerce Department's Bureau of Economic Analysis. See www.bea.gov/newsreleases/national/gdp/2016/pdf/gdp4q15_3rd.pdf.

4. Hamilton wrote: "It is well known (and particular examples, in the course of this report, will be cited) that certain nations grant bounties on the exportation of particular commodities, to enable their own workmen to undersell and supplant all competitors, in the countries to which those commodities are sent. Hence the undertakers of a new manufacture have to contend, not only with the natural disadvantages of a new undertaking, but with the gratuities and remunerations which other governments bestow. To be enabled to contend with success, it is evident, that the interference and aid of their own government are indispensable." Alexander Hamilton, *Alexander Hamilton's Famous Report on Manufactures Made to Congress December 5, 1791, In His Capacity as Secretary of the Treasury*, in Harold C. Syrett, ed., *The Papers of Alexander Hamilton*, vol. 10, December 1791–January 1792 (New York: Columbia University Press, 1966), 124–230. (An online version of Hamilton's fourth draft of the text, showing his revisions, is available at founders.archives.gov/documents/Hamilton/01-10-02-0001-0006.)

5. In our era, economics has become a highly ideological, even partisan, discipline, but Hamilton did not characterize his views on the necessity of government subsidies for manufacturing with an ideological label that we would recognize today. The industrial revolution was in too early a stage for Hamilton to see himself as a capitalist or a socialist or a Marxist (*capitalist* in English dates from the 1780s; the two other terms from decades later). One of the foundational texts of modern economics, Adam Smith's *The Wealth of Nations*, which describes the mechanics of an assembly line and of a market system, had been published only fifteen years before Hamilton wrote his *Report*. Yet Hamilton saw clearly that manufacturing and government subsidies were of necessity intertwined. (The rise of economics as a modern intellectual discipline in fact parallels the rise of manufacturing. Robert Heilbroner's *The Worldly Philosophers: The Lives, Times and Ideas of the Great Economic Thinkers*, originally published in 1953, offers an accessible survey of the development of economic ideas, beginning with Smith's.)

6. The authorization of the Ex-Im Bank (as it is called in economics jargon) was scheduled to expire on September 30, 2014, just four months after the NAM meeting. Before that deadline, Congress approved a nine-month extension, and then approved full reauthorization on December 4, 2015—and for a longer-than-usual period: until September 30, 2019. Among other activities, the Ex-Im Bank guarantees repayment of commercial loans obtained by overseas customers to purchase merchandise manufactured in the United States. Or manufacturers in the United States provide financing to pay for merchandise they export, and then if a customer abroad fails to pay for the goods received, the Ex-Im Bank reimburses the manufacturer from federal tax revenues. Without that guarantee, overseas customers would be charged higher interest rates for loans, if they could get them at all. As a result, they would be less likely to purchase American-made products. The bottom line would be fewer exports resulting in less factory output in the United States and a bigger trade deficit than the one that already exists. Boeing, for example, has been a big supporter of the Ex-Im Bank, which guarantees repayment of loans obtained by overseas airlines to purchase airliners manufactured by Boeing.

7. The auto bailout team appointed by the Obama administration consisted of the same three men who had served on President Obama's task force on manufacturing. They were Steven Rattner, the Wall Street financier; Ron Bloom, the USW official who went to Wall Street; and Gene Sperling, the former director of Obama's National Economic Council. As for GM, the federal government invested $49.5 billion in the auto company through the purchase of GM stock. *Time*, quoting from a government report in its April 13, 2014, edition, reported that "U.S. taxpayers lost more than $11.2 billion as a result of the federal bailout of General Motors. . . . The $11.2-billion loss included an $826-million write-off in March 2014 from government investments in the 'Old GM' before the company's 2009 bankruptcy. . . . [T]he government's investment [in GM] was converted to a 61 percent equity stake in the company. The Treasury gradually sold off its stock in GM, selling its last shares in December 2013." See Sam Frizell, "General Motors Bailout Cost Taxpayers $11.2 Billion," *Time*, Apr. 30, 2014.

Fiat purchased all of Chrysler's remaining equity in 2014. See George Schultze, "The Story Behind Chrysler and Fiat, and Why the Stock Is So Cheap," *Forbes*, Jan. 7, 2014.

8. Sperling served as deputy director of the National Economic Council (NEC) from 1993 to 1996 and then as director from 1996 to 2001, both terms under President Clinton. President Obama named him NEC director in January 2011. He left the administration in 2014.

9. See "The Case for a Manufacturing Renaissance, Prepared Remarks by Gene Sperling, The Brookings Institution, July 25, 2013," www.whitehouse.gov/sites/default/files/docs/the_case_for_a_manufacturing_renaissance_gene _sperling_7-25-2013_final_p. . . . pdf.

10. Ron Bloom joined the Obama administration in February 2009, a month after the president took office, and served until August 2011. His posts included assistant to the president for manufacturing policy, senior advisor to the secretary of the Treasury, a member of the Presidential Task Force on the Auto Industry, and senior counselor to President Obama for Manufacturing Policy.

11. The Electric Home and Farm Authority (EHFA), a federal agency, was created to finance and guarantee installment payments that consumers made to purchase electric stoves, refrigerators, washing machines, clothes irons, and other appliances. Separately, the Roosevelt administration arranged with GE to mass-produce the necessary low-priced appliances. The low-cost electricity to run them, in turn, came from the Tennessee Valley Authority and other hydroelectric projects built by the federal government. See Jordan A. Schwarz, *The New Dealers: Power Politics in the Age of Roosevelt* (New York: Knopf, 1993), 238–39, and Louis Uchitelle, *The Disposable American: Layoffs and Their Consequences* (New York: Knopf, 2006), 40–41.

12. A state-by-state survey conducted by LoanBack (www.loanback.com /category/usury-laws-by-state) and dated March 2, 2011, showed that usury ceilings that once were less than 10 percent were above that level in many cases, if they existed at all. No ceiling existed, for example, in Utah and South Carolina, while in New York and New Jersey the usury limit was 16 percent, in Massachusetts 20 percent, in Kansas 15 percent, in Connecticut 12 percent, in Florida 18 percent, and in Oklahoma 10 percent for nonconsumer loans. Michigan's limit was a relatively low 7 percent, an encouragement for manufacturers in this industrial state. Several other states have similarly low usury ceilings.

13. The annual trade deficit exceeded $100 billion in 1984, the first triple-digit deficit since 1960. Until the 1970s, the trade balance had been mostly

in surplus. After 1975, it was not in surplus for the rest of the century, nor in the first sixteen years of the twenty-first century. See Census Bureau, *U.S. Trade in Goods and Services—Balance of Payments (BOP) Basis.* Go to www .census.gov, then search for U.S. Trade in Goods and Services, Balance of Payments Basis.

14. See Louis Uchitelle, "Taxes Help Foot the Payrolls as States Vie for Employers," *New York Times*, Aug. 11, 1998.

15. See the World Bank's "Manufacturing, Value Added (% of GDP)" table at data.worldbank.org/indicator/NV.IND.MANF.ZS, which covers the period 1995–2014. Germany, the European colossus, has devoted 23 percent of its economic output to manufacturing all through the twenty-first century. China and South Korea are each at 30 percent. Even Mexico is well ahead of the United States, at 18 percent, partly because it hosts the factories of numerous U.S.-based multinationals.

16. See Andy Sharman, Jude Webber, and Kana Inagaki, "Ford Investment Highlights Mexico's Booming Carmaking Sector," *Financial Times*, Apr. 16, 2015: "Mexico's share of North American [car] production is expected to rise to a quarter by 2022, and some analysts say it would not be absurd to think of the country overtaking the US for the number of cars made. The US last year [in 2014] made 11.5m[illion] vehicles, compared to more than 3m[illion] in Mexico." The article reports that Ford was "poised to give Mexico's carmaking sector a fresh boost . . . with the announcement of $2.5b[illio]n in manufacturing investments" in auto factory production, specifically the expansion of an engine factory in the state of Chihuahua and the construction of a new gearbox factory in Guanajuato.

17. For example, according to the *St. Louis Business Journal*, the publicly funded St. Louis Regional Convention and Sports Complex Authority had by April 2015 spent "at least $773,811 in tax money on the effort to build an NFL [National Football League] stadium on the Mississippi riverfront just north of downtown." The new stadium, still in the planning stages at the time, was expected to cost up to $1 billion to construct, according to the *Journal*. The outlay went for naught: the St. Louis team abruptly decided in 2016 to relocate to Los Angeles, depriving the stadium of its high-profile anchor occupant. See Jacob Kirn, "Dome Board Has Spent $774,000 in Public Money on New Stadium," *St. Louis Business Journal*, Apr. 29, 2015, www.bizjournals.com

/stlouis/news/2015/04/29/dome-board-has-spent-774-000-in-public-money
-on.html.

18. See Louis Uchitelle, "Unions Yield on Pay Scales to Preserve Jobs," *New York Times*, Nov. 19, 2010.

19. Ibid.

20. Ibid. Less than a month earlier, Barrett had run as the Democratic candidate for governor of Wisconsin, losing the election to Scott Walker, his Republican opponent.

21. Whirlpool paid $21 a share, or a total of $1.7 billion, for Maytag. The Department of Justice, after considering the obvious antitrust issue—potential damage to consumers from lowered competition—approved the merger in March 2006, nearly a year after Whirlpool made its initial offer of $17 a share to purchase its smaller rival. Whirlpool argued successfully that the merger still left such powerful competitors in the manufacture of appliances as GE, Frigidaire, LG, Samsung, and Bosch.

22. For background, see Louis Uchitelle, "Is There (Middle Class) Life After Maytag?," *New York Times*, Aug. 26, 2007; and "The Wage That Meant Middle Class," *New York Times*, Apr. 20, 2008.

23. The American Society of Civil Engineers estimated in October of 2014 that the nation's public infrastructure required repairs and upgrades costing $3.6 trillion between 2014 and 2020 to function efficiently.

24. For example, the Grand Coulee Dam and the Bonneville Power Administration dams and hydroelectric generators, all built on the Columbia River in Washington State by the federal government, generate electric power at reasonable prices, making possible aluminum manufacturing in the Northwest and aircraft manufacturing at the Boeing factory complex near Seattle, among other industrial activities. The Tennessee Valley Authority provides the same abundant and inexpensive electricity in the southeast. And government has played a big role in financing and operating nuclear power plants. For background and context, see Jordan A. Schwarz, *The New Dealers: Power Politics in the Age of Roosevelt* (New York: Knopf, 1993).

25. Revere Copper dates back to 1801 and to Paul Revere, a pioneer in the production of rolled sheet copper that was used to sheath the hulls of naval vessels, according to the company's website. After Revere's death, "generations of Revere's descendants remained active in the business. The copper works

founded in 1801 continues today as Revere Copper Products, Inc. in Rome, New York, making it one of the oldest manufacturing companies in the United States. See "Revere Copper: Our Story," www.reverecopper.com/about-us.

26. According to PitchBook Data, private equity firms bought control of three hundred U.S. manufacturing operations in 2010, 331 in 2011, 471 in 2012, 474 in 2013, and 490 in 2014. In nearly all such transactions, the equity firm borrows money to make the purchase and then requires the company it purchased to repay the debt. The repayment, in turn, uses up sales revenue that might have gone to profit or to the purchase of new machinery or to expansion or to wage increases.

27. See Louis Uchitelle, "Subsidies Aid Rebirth in U.S. Manufacturing," *New York Times*, May 10, 2012.

28. See Robert Pollin and Heidi Garrett-Peltier, "The U.S. Employment Effects of Military and Domestic Spending Priorities," Institute for Policy Studies/Political Economy Research Institute/Women's Action for New Directions, October 2007, www.comw.org/pda/fulltext/pollin-Garrett-Peltier.pdf. Additional information on federal weapons spending came from a telephone interview on April 22, 2015, with Richard Aboulafia, a military weapons analyst with the Teal Group, near Washington, D.C. See also Louise Story's three-part *New York Times* series on tax incentives and subsidies in various industries, including manufacturing. The series, starting each day on page one, ran in the *Times* on December 2, 3, and 4, 2012 (the online publication dates, as is usual at the *Times*, are all one day earlier). The stories were headlined: "The Empty Promise of Tax Incentives" (online as "As Companies Seek Tax Deals, Governments Pay High Price"); "Lines Blur as Texas Gives Industries a Bonanza"; and "Michigan Town Woos Hollywood, but Ends Up with a Bit Part."

29. Two famous historical examples of vital public infrastructure, built with subsidies and linked to manufacturing as well as to the public's needs, were the Erie Canal and the transcontinental railroad. In 1817, DeWitt Clinton, the Republican governor of New York State, initiated construction of the canal, financing it largely with state-sponsored bonds. After its completion eight years later, freight could move by water between New York City and ports on the Great Lakes. Manufacturers soon set up factories served by this vast waterway, and the New York state legislature, in addition, "made some twenty-eight major loans to manufacturers, claiming 'the establishment of useful

manufactures is clearly connected with the public weal.'" See Jeff Madrick, *The Case for Big Government* (Princeton: Princeton University Press, 2009), 40.

As for the transcontinental railroad, the subsidies were authorized by the Pacific Railroad Act, enacted by Congress and signed into law on July 1, 1862, by President Lincoln. That act authorized payment of a federal "subsidy of $16,600 a mile on the plains, and from $32,000 to $48,000 a mile through the mountains" to the builders of the railroad, which connected the Pacific Ocean and the Missouri River. In return, the government secured from those who constructed and owned the railroad "the use of the same for Postal, Military and other purposes." This initial legislation turned out not to be enough to satisfy the promoters jockeying to build the railroad. So in 1864, Congress increased the subsidy, and Lincoln agreed. Construction began in 1866, once the Civil War had ended. See George R. Leighton, *Five Cities* (New York: Harper and Brothers, 1939), 150–53. Once it had been completed, factories appeared along the railroad's route, and along spur lines that branched out from the main line.

30. My understanding, based on numerous public statements, is that all government entities in the United States, federal, state, and local, maintain policies that mandate the purchase of manufactured goods that have been made or assembled at factories located in the United States. As a result of these "buy America" practices, the purchase of imported goods is kept to a minimum at all levels of government.

31. Anders, born in 1933, was a U.S. Air Force officer and an astronaut; he worked for GE and Textron before moving to General Dynamics, where he became chairman and CEO in 1991. He retired as CEO in 1993 but continued as chairman until May 1994.

32. See Louis Uchitelle, "Arms Makers: Rather Fight Than Switch" *New York Times*, Sept. 20, 1992.

33. Ibid.

34. Summaries of General Dynamics quarterly reports are available in press releases going back to 2010 at www.generaldynamics.com/news/press-releases.

5. Offshoring and How It Could Be Reversed: The Challenges

1. While President Obama publicly supported TPP, Congress delayed a vote on the treaty as election day approached in 2016.

2. See two GM press releases: "General Motors Sets Sales Records in China," Dec. 3, 2014, media.chevrolet.com/media/me/en/gm/news.detail .html/content/Pages/news/cn/en/2014/Dec/1203_sales.html; and "GM Sells First Half Record 1.72 Million Vehicles in China," July 6, 2015, media.gm.com /media/me/en/gm/news.detail.html/content/Pages/news/cn/en/2015/july /0706_sales.html.

3. See the Reshoring Initiative's website, www.reshorenow.org/companies -reshoring.

4. Ibid.

5. See www.reshorenow.org. While the slide file singles out three hundred companies, the Reshoring Initiative said, on its website, that as of February 2016, there were "over 1,300 documented cases of companies that have chosen to manufacture in the U.S. instead of offshore." The 1,300 included companies that considered putting a manufacturing operation abroad and then decided against doing so, as well as companies that transferred production abroad and then reshored it.

6. Ibid.

7. See the Reshoring Initiative's Aviator Sunglasses case study at www .reshorenow.org/content/companies_reshoring/Cases_only_2-20.pdf.

8. Ibid.

9. Telephone interview with Greg Wathen, Sept. 3, 2015.

10. Interview with Bloom in New York on July 22, 2015. See chapter 4, footnote 10, for Bloom's background.

11. Ibid.

12. See chapter 1, note 13.

13. Bloom's successor in the administration was Jason Miller, who came from the Boston Consulting Group and had less career experience in manufacturing than Bloom.

14. See chapter 1, note 13.

15. Telephone interview with Alan Beggerow, May 4, 2016.

16. Ibid.

17. Only one other company, Pratt & Whitney, makes similar engines in the United States, mainly at factories in the Northeast.

18. The interview took place in a conference room at the Evendale factory on Sept. 9, 2015.

19. While Athans mentioned twelve countries, she listed nine in our Sept. 10, 2015, interview. Besides the United States, they were China, Brazil, Hungary, France, Italy, Canada, Great Britain, and Mexico.

20. Interview, Sept. 10, 2015 (see note 19).

21. Ibid.

22. Ibid.

23. See chapter 1, note 19.

24. Interview, Sept. 10, 2015 (see note 19).

25. Douglas A. Fraser, president of the UAW from 1977 to 1983, is a rare example of a union leader serving as a board member for a major American corporation. He was a director of the Chrysler Corporation from 1980 to 1984. Chrysler named him to the board after he persuaded UAW members to lobby Congress on behalf of the $1.2 billion loan guarantee that saved Chrysler from bankruptcy, but only after the UAW under Fraser endorsed the loan guarantee. Fraser also negotiated labor concessions from Ford in 1982, during a recession that hurt sales. In the end, his UAW members at Chrysler accepted a three-dollar-per-hour wage reduction and the lifting of restrictions on layoffs, which allowed the company to shed nearly fifty thousand jobs, or half its workforce. The same concessions went to General Motors and Ford, as Fraser sought to keep wages uniform across the Big Three. Some in the union movement, however, criticized Fraser for undoing a thirty-year truce between labor and management under which the auto manufacturers had agreed to pattern bargaining and to periodic cost-of-living increases.

26. See Uchitelle's *The Disposable American: Layoffs and Their Consequences* (New York: Alfred A. Knopf, 2006), 11. See also Davis's *New York Times* obituary: David Kocieniewski, "Donald W. Davis, Who Headed Stanley Works, Dies at 89," Sept. 17, 2010.

27. Telephone interview Oct. 16, 2015, with Ayers, from his home in New Hampshire.

Afterword

1. See "The Alcoa Story," which includes an abbreviated version of the full tale, at www.alcoa.com/usa/en/alcoa_usa/history.asp.

2. See David McCullough, *The Wright Brothers* (New York: Simon & Schuster, 2015), 87.

3. The Department of Commerce Bureau of Economic Analysis tracks the share of imports from the overseas factories of American multinationals, but infrequently. The BEA published the most recent number in 2013, and that report covered activity only through 2011.

4. See Louis Uchitelle, "How Two-Tier Union Contracts Became Labor's Undoing," *The Nation*, Feb. 6, 2013. My research for this article includes notes from telephone interviews conducted on Nov. 13 and 14, 2012. See also Bill Vlasic and Mary M. Chapmannov, "U.A.W. Contracts Change Math for Detroit Automakers," *New York Times*, Nov. 24, 2015.

5. See Louis Uchitelle, "U.S. Businesses Loosen Link to Mother Country," *New York Times*, May 21, 1989.

6. Mariana Mazzucato, *The Entrepreneurial State: Debunking Public vs. Private Sector Myths* (rev. ed., New York: PublicAffairs, 2015 [London, U.K.: Anthem, 2013]).

7. Ibid., 210.

8. See Bureau of Labor Statistics, "Establishment Data: Employees on Non-Farm Payrolls by Industry Sector and Selected Industry Detail," www.bls.gov /webapps/legacy/cesbtab1.htm.

Index

About the Author

Louis Uchitelle covered economics and labor issues for the *New York Times* for twenty-five years. Before that, as a foreign correspondent for the Associated Press, he covered the American occupation of the Dominican Republic in the 1960s and the rise of a guerrilla movement in Argentina. He is also the author of *The Disposable American: Layoffs and Their Consequences*. He and his wife, Joan, live in Scarsdale, New York, as do their two daughters and their husbands, along with four grandchildren.

Other Titles of Interest from The New Press

Stayin' Alive: The 1970s and the Last Days of the Working Class by Jefferson Cowie

Wage Theft in America: Why Millions of Working Americans Are Not Getting Paid—And What We Can Do About It by Kim Bobo

Were You Born on the Wrong Continent? How the European Model Can Help You Get a Life by Thomas Geoghegan

Which Side Are You On? Trying to Be for Labor When It's Flat on Its Back by Thomas Geoghegan

Working: People Talk About What They Do All Day and How They Feel About What They Do by Studs Terkel

Celebrating 25 Years of Independent Publishing

Thank you for reading this book published by The New Press. The New Press is a nonprofit, public interest publisher celebrating its twenty-fifth anniversary in 2017. New Press books and authors play a crucial role in sparking conversations about the key political and social issues of our day.

We hope you enjoyed this book and that you will stay in touch with The New Press. Here are a few ways to stay up to date with our books, events, and the issues we cover:

- Sign up at www.thenewpress.com/subscribe to receive updates on New Press authors and issues and to be notified about local events.
- Like us on Facebook: www.facebook.com/newpressbooks.
- Follow us on Twitter: www.twitter.com/thenewpress.

Please consider buying New Press books for yourself; for friends and family; or to donate to schools, libraries, community centers, prison libraries, and other organizations involved with the issues our authors write about.

The New Press is a 501(c)(3) nonprofit organization. You can also support our work with a tax-deductible gift by visiting www.thenewpress.com/donate.